PABLO PICASSO

ediciones polígrafa

masterpieces

PABLO PICASSO

CONTENTS

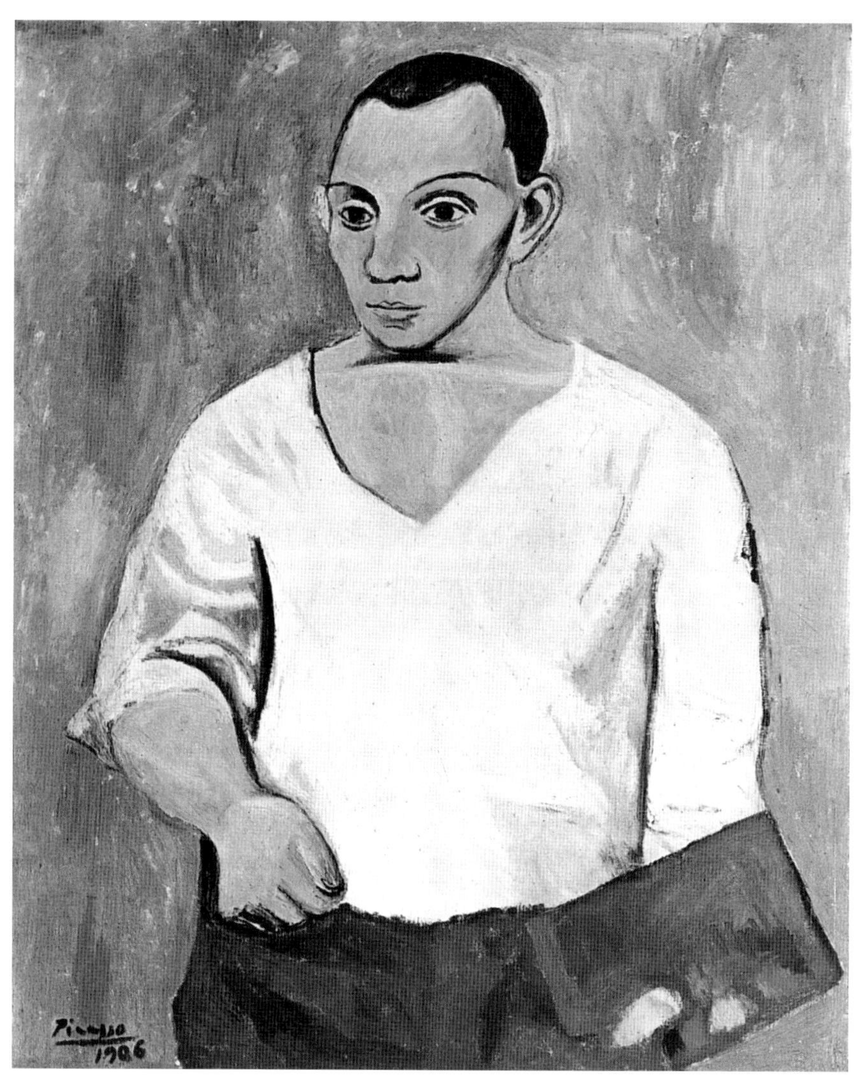

SELF-PORTRAIT WITH A PALETTE, 1906.
Oil on canvas, 92x73 cm.
The Philadelphia Museum of Art,
A. E. Gallatin Collection.

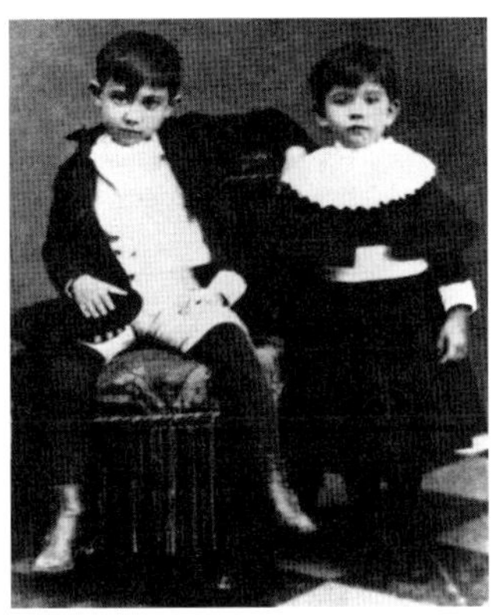

PABLO PICASSO AND CUBISM

No one disputes the fact that Pablo Picasso is among the most important masters of the twentieth century, a reputation bestowed upon him as early as the 1920s, when Cubism was already well known. In his life and work he personifies perfectly the image of the modern artist: he chose the Bohemian lifestyle at the beginning of the century, having scorned the certainty of a conventional and academic career for which he demonstrated himself to be perfectly qualified; he possessed overwhelming and almost mythic vitality, symbolized in the figure of the minotaur ever present in his work; and he had exceptional natural talent that lends his paintings that sense of ease expressed in the famous words: "I do not seek, I find."

BREAKING NEW GROUND

But Picasso's work would not occupy the place it does today unless one adds to those qualities his determination to break new ground on the path that modern painting had been exploring since the time of Edouard Manet and the Impressionists. The modernist objective—which Picasso made his own—was to find a method of representing reality within the superficial condition of painting which has its own coherent, internal logic. Picasso took the definitive step in achieving this goal in 1907, when he completed *Les Demoiselles d'Avignon*, and thus opened the doors to Cubism.

Cubism is a specifically pictorial revolution that has little to do with the physical or philosophical theories with which critics have at times sought to establish direct relationships. Paul Cézanne had already introduced spatial distortions in his still lifes, seeking to provide the viewer with the maximum information possible about the painted object. To that precedent may be added the profound impression

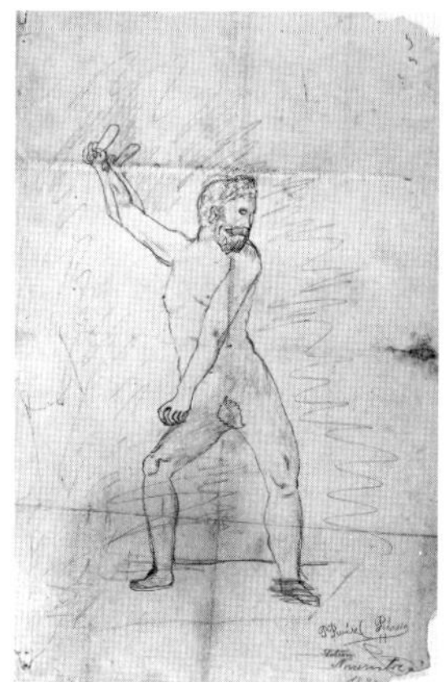 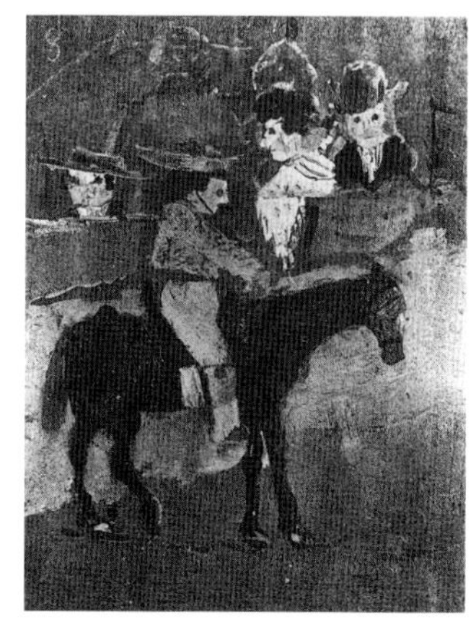

made on Picasso by primitive Iberian sculpture and African masks
which revealed modes of synthetic and non-naturalistic representation
unknown in the European tradition. Incorporating those lessons in
Les Demoiselles, the painter from Málaga crossed the threshold
between painting things as one sees them and representing what
one knows about them. Until World War I, both Picasso and painter
Georges Braque explored the possibilities of that new idea, unfolding
and juxtaposing different planes and views of the subject on the
surface of the canvas.

HERCULES WITH A CLUB, 1890.
The artist was not even ten
years old when he began this
academic study.

PICADOR, c. 1890. The first
example of Picasso's preference
for bullfighting subjects.

A NEW ORDER

As a result of that exploration, the Cubist painting generates its own
order, independent of the order of reality perceived by the senses. This
order extends not only to the objects represented, but to the depiction
of the empty space between them. The declaration that the Cubist
painter paints an object as though moving around it should not be
taken literally. Nor is the artist merely seeking to introduce time as a
fourth dimension in the painting. Instead, the painter begins with an
idea, a mental image of the object, in order to reproduce it according
to strictly pictorial laws. It is futile to attempt to *reconstruct* an object
in a Cubist painting as one would compose a solid geometric body in
three dimensions based on a two-dimensional diagram. What is
indeed possible is to *recognize* it, and for that purpose the painter
leaves a series of figurative clues which the viewer can use as a guide.

THE PAINTING AS OBJECT

But Cubism was to go even farther in its manipulation of the painted
object. Its discoveries permit the establishment of a new relationship
between painting and reality: what one perceives as a whole can be

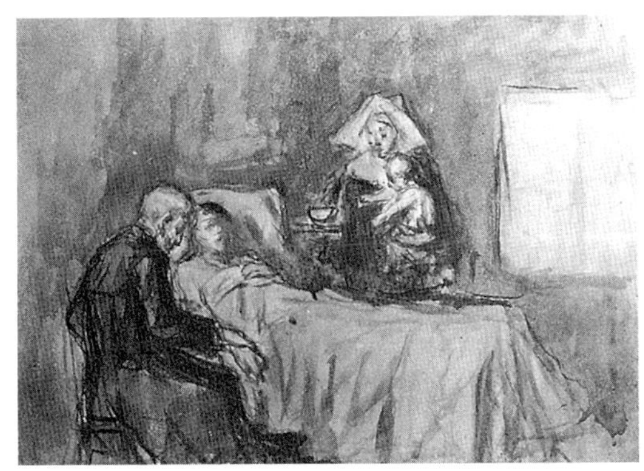

depicted in its parts; what is seen as concave can be painted in a convex fashion, and vice versa. From 1912 onward, first Picasso and then Braque began to integrate into their works scraps of colored or printed paper, cigarette packages, and other elements from their daily surroundings, inventing what is known as collage and *papier collé*. In this purification of Cubist expression the terms of portrayal are altered: it is no longer necessary to start with the object in order to form the structure of the painting. Rather, beginning with a scheme of drawing and color, representative elements are introduced onto the canvas—whether painted, glued on, or superimposed—to piece together or synthesize the composition. Thus we reach the mature phase of Cubism, which is commonly called Synthetic Cubism, as opposed to "primitive" Cubism, in which the process can be said to be, on the contrary, analytical, because the object is broken down on the canvas into a composite of parts.

At this point, the painting moves beyond being a representation of reality to being an element added to it: what the Cubists called the *tableau-objet* (picture-object). Thus the circle closes, and Cubism, from then on, becomes the matrix of almost all avant-garde expression, somewhat like the basic grammar of an interdisciplinary, formal language, valid in its universal application to the fields of art, design, architecture, and industry. Although Picasso shares the credit for the development of Cubism with Georges Braque and, to a lesser degree, with Juan Gris and other painters and theoreticians of the movement, after 1907 the key steps were always taken by Picasso, which explains his reputation as the first truly modern painter.

A UNIVERSAL ART

Although Cubism is the cornerstone of Picasso's art, his career transcends school. It is often said that his artistic evolution summarizes all the

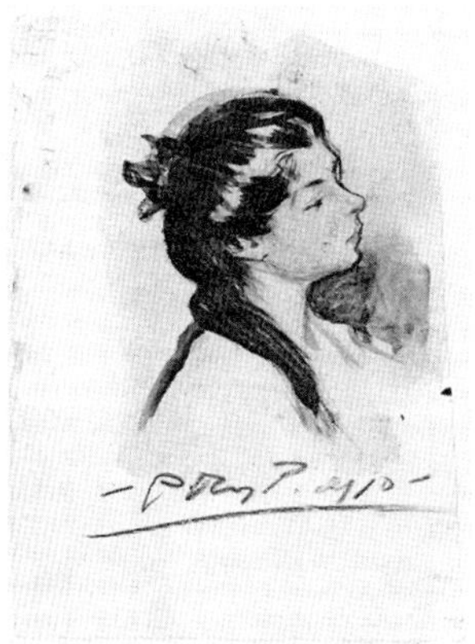

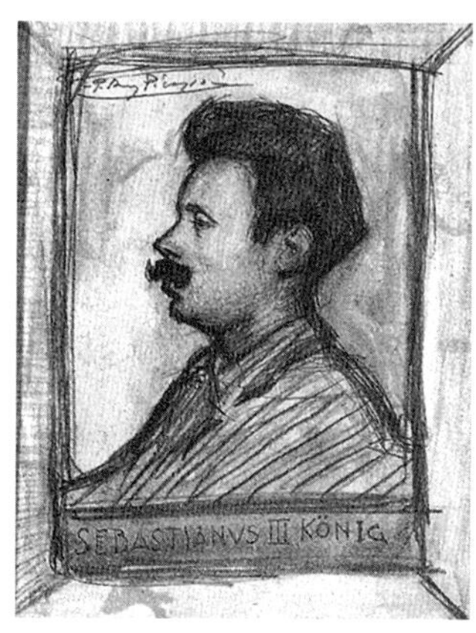

trends of modern art. This statement is only partially true, but it gives some idea of his capacity to interpret and convey the spirit of his time; the universal and emblematic value of *Guernica* as an expression of the horror of war speaks for itself. Picasso's sphere of influence is vast and informs our understanding of both the historical avant-garde and abstract painting after 1945. Over time, his discoveries were appropriated by him and by others in contexts quite different from their original applications. This explains why he is the pivotal figure of twentieth-century painting, and likewise suggests why his work—even the late, marginal, or seemingly minor—forever retains an artistic vitality that few can claim for themselves.

PORTRAIT OF LOLA, 1899. The influence of fin-de-siècle Barcelona can be seen in the elegant ease of technique in this drawing.

PORTRAIT OF SEBASTIÀ JUNYER VIDAL, 1900. This Germanic-style portrait reflects the Wagnerian fashion of the time.

PABLO PICASSO, 1881-1973

Pablo Ruiz Picasso, who once his career as a painter was established would sign only with his mother's surname, was born in Málaga, Spain, into an artistic family. His father, José Ruiz Blasco, earned his living as a drawing teacher, first in Málaga and then in La Coruña and Barcelona. Although Picaso began his study of the fine arts in La Coruña, it was in Barcelona, where the family moved in 1895, that he completed his formal training and began his career. His extraordinary artistic talents were soon apparent, and honorable mention his work *Science and Charity* obtained at a national exhibition in 1897 seemed to augur for him a brilliant future as an academic painter.

THE BOHEMIAN YEARS

Instead of following the path of academic painting, however, Picasso immersed himself in the Bohemian life of Barcelona at the beginning

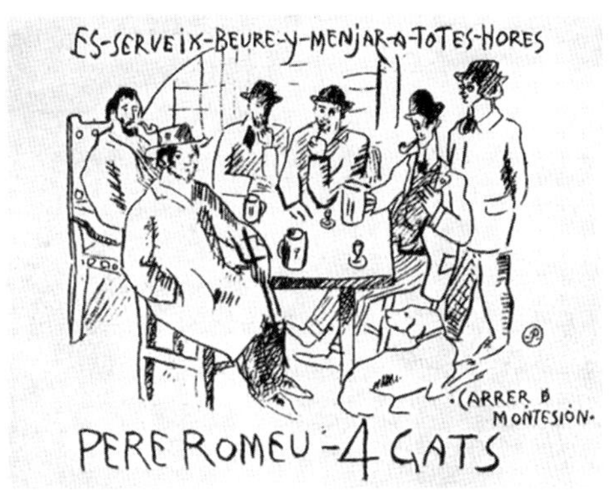

of the century. At that time the Catalan capital was an artistic center of great vitality, where *modernisme* in architecture and the decorative arts coexisted with the major trends of the European art scene: the poetic taste for Symbolism, embodied in painters like Modest Urgell, and the new, *plein air* painting that Ramón Casas and Santiago Rusiñol had imported from Paris. Picasso frequented Els Quatre Gats tavern, where he met all the Catalan artists of the day. In 1900 he made his first trip to Paris with his friend Carles Casagemas. One year later, he had his first French exhibition, and in 1904 he took up residence in the legendary Bateau-Lavoir in the district of Montmartre. He spent this first stage of his career—the so-called Blue and Rose Periods which lasted until 1906— traveling between Paris and Barcelona. In the paintings of this era the figures, drawn with the mastery for which Picasso is well known, stand out against monochromatic backgrounds of blue and rose. Predominant in this period of Picasso's work is the influence of the Catalan painter Isidro Nonell, with his preference for allegorical scenes of the starker aspects of human existence.

CUBISM

An interest in Iberian sculpture and the African masks in the Musée du Trocadéro marks a new direction in Picasso's work in 1906 (*Self-Portrait with a Palette, Portrait of Gertrude Stein*). During that year and the next the artist worked on *Les Demoiselles d'Avignon*, truly the point of departure for Cubism. In the paintings completed in 1908 in Horta de Ebro, geometric and faceted volumes are spread across the surface of the canvas, signaling the first steps in the new movement. The development of this movement took place between 1900 and 1914, the period when Picasso worked closely with Georges Braques, that he met in 1907 through the poet Guillaume

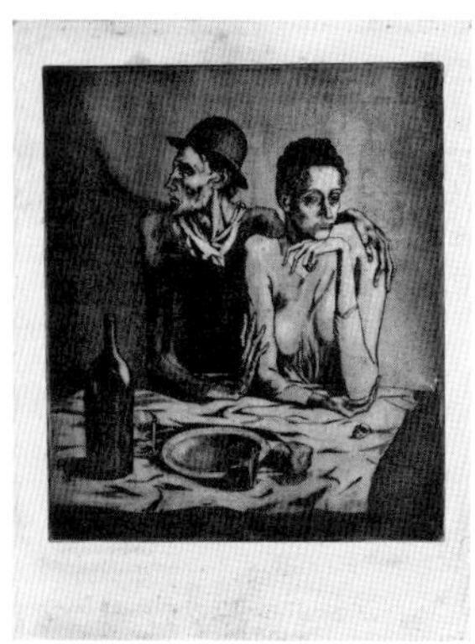 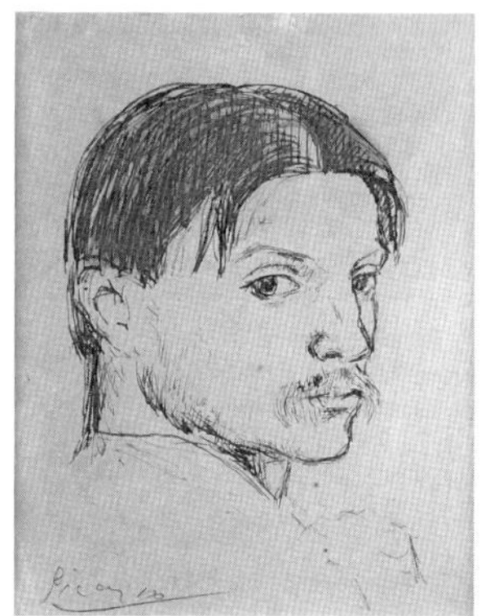

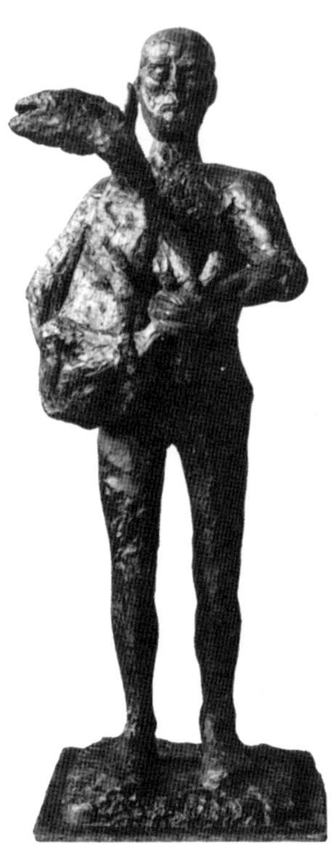

Apollinaire. That collaboration purified this new language and produced new modes of expression such as collage and *papier collé*, which Picasso began to employ about 1912. These new techniques established a new relationship between painting and perceived reality, constituting a pivotal moment in modern painting.

In the further refinement of the new artistic method that is commonly known as Synthetic Cubism, the collaboration between Picasso and Serge Diaghilev's Ballets Russes is of great importance. In 1916, through his connection with Jean Cocteau, Picasso designed the sets for the ballet *Parade*, with music by Erik Satie; this was the starting point for a certain decorative dimension of Cubism. During this period Picasso met ballerina Olga Koklova, whom he married in 1918 and who was the mother of his first son. The painter had previously relationships with Fernande Olivier and Marcelle Humbert, the Eva in the first Cubist canvases.

A CENTURY OF WARS

During the period between the two World Wars, Picasso continued to explore the possibilities of Cubism through painting, collage, and sculpture, occasionally returning to a classical, Mediterranean figurative style (*Three Women at the Spring*, 1921). The introduction of fantastic subjects captured the attention of the Surrealists, who greatly respected him. The Spanish Civil War was a new milestone in the artist's life and work; Picasso embraced the Republican cause and accepted the position of Director of the Prado Museum in Madrid. From this position he was able to contribute to safeguarding Spain's national artistic treasures. In 1937, German planes supporting the rebel forces under General Francisco Franco bombed the town of Guernica, causing a full-scale massacre of a civilian population. Picasso's profound shock and horror provoked by this act of slaughter

THE FRUGAL REPAST, 1904. This is one of the artist's first attempts in the field of engraving.

Beginning with the large SELF-PORTRAIT of 1901, Picasso frequently made self-portraits. This sketch was done in Paris, a year after the famous 1901 painting with which it bears an evident relationship.

MAN WITH KID, 1944. Picasso's sculptures are considered among the greatest creations in this medium of the twentieth century.

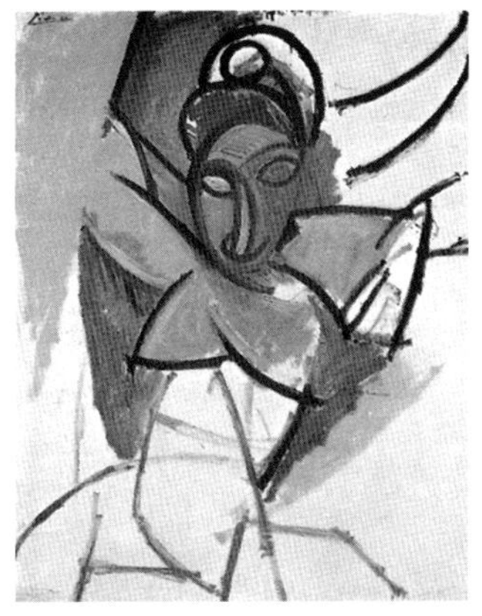

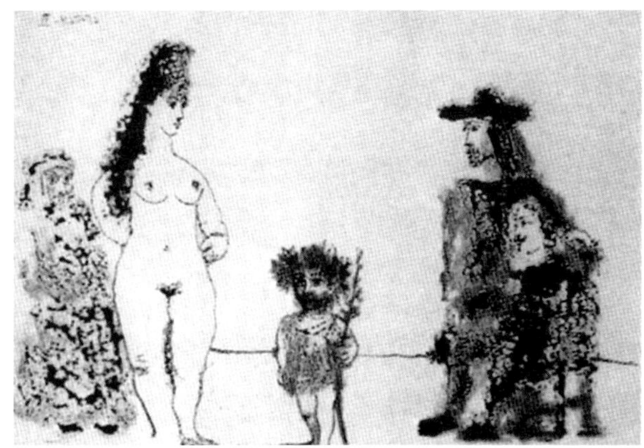

resulted in *Guernica*, which was shown in the Spanish Pavilion of the Paris World's Fair that same year. In time it became the most famous and most reproduced painting of the twentieth century. The influence of *Guernica* lends a certain expressionism to all of the artist's work of the 1930s, adding a new dimension to the Cubist treatment of the human figure. These were the years of Picasso's relationship with Dora Maar, who followed on from Marie-Thérèse Walter, the mother of Picasso's second child.

THE FINAL YEARS

At the end of World War II Picasso took up residence in the south of France, an area he had frequented since the 1920s. His artistic vitality led him to ceramics and sculpture which he practiced regularly throughout his career, to the point of being considered one of the great sculptors of the century. His abundant output of graphic work also deserves, on its own merits, a privileged place in the history of modern art. Picasso's last two amorous relationships, with Françoise Gilot (with whom he had two more children) and Jacqueline Roque (whom he married in 1961 and with whom he remained until his death), provided him with the stability that made the astonishing productivity of his later career possible. In those last years, the artist employed all the resources he had discovered his long career to create in the course of paintings an extraordinary freedom, filtering through it, indirectly, aspects of his personal life. Picasso's legendary Dionysian vitality remained with him until his death in 1973, at the height of his creative powers.

1881 Birth of Picasso in Málaga on October 25. In 1885 his sister Lola is born; and in 1887, his sister Concepción.

1891 September: the Picasso family moves to La Coruña.

1895 Death of Concepción. Drawings and paintings: *Beggar in a Cap. The Barefoot Girl.* Exhibition in the back room of a shop. Summer in Málaga. September: the family moves to Barcelona. Picasso enters the Llotja School of Fine Arts, at which his father teaches drawing.

1896 *The First Communion,* shown at the Barcelona Fine Arts Exhibition. Academic and free works. Self-portraits. Acquires a studio at no 4 carrer de la Plata, but lives with his family at no. 3. carrer de la Mercè.

1897 *Science and Charity* is awarded an Honorable Mention at the Madrid Fine Arts exhibition. Foundation of the 4 Gats. Autumn: moves to Madrid. Studies at the Academy of San Fernando and in the Prado.

1898 Returns to Barcelona in the spring. Spends the summer with Manuel Pallarès at Horta de Ebro, most of the time in a cave in the "Ports" or Passes of the Maestrat range of mountains. Self-portraits. "Everything I know, I learnt in Horta de Ebro." End of the Spanish-American War.

1899 Returns to Barcelona. Attends drawing classes at the Cercle Artístic. Acquires a studio in carrer d'Escudellers Blancs. *Portrait of Josep Cardona.* Meets Sabartés. *Lola behind a Window.*

1900 Shares a studio with Carles Casagemas at no. 17 Riera de Sant Joan. February: exhibits at the 4 Gats. Many portraits: Soto, Sabartés, Reventós, Vidal Ventosa, Pitxot, etc. October: first visit to Paris, with Casagemas. *Le Moulin de la Galette.* Signs a contract with Pere Manyac. Christmas in Barcelona.

1901 New Year in Málaga. February: journey to Madrid. Founds the review *Arte Joven* with F. d'A. Soler. May: passes through Barcelona. June: second visit to Paris, with Jaume Andreu. Exhibition at the Galerie Vollard. "Pre-fauvisme". Meets Max Jacob. *Harlequin Leaning on the Table.* Breaks with Manyac. Beginning of the Blue Period. *Large Blue Self-portrait.*

1902 January: returns to Barcelona. Takes a studio in carrer Nou, with Rocarol. *Drunk Woman Sleeping* (or *The Absinthe Drinker), Whores in a Bar.* Autumn: third visit to Paris, with Rocarol. Stays at the Hôtel du Maroc, suffering cold and hunger.

1903 January: returns to Barcelona, and to his studio in Riera de Sant Joan. *Life, Poor People on the Seashore.* Autumn: moves to a studio at no. 28 in carrer Comerç.

1904 Blue portraits. April: moves to Paris with S. Junyer-Vidal. Moves into the Bateau-Lavoir. Meets Fernande Olivier. *The Couple, The Frugal Repast* (etching), *Woman with the Raven.*

1905 Blue-rose or Rose Period: *Acrobat on a Ball.* Summer: visits Holland. *The Three Dutchwomen. The Tumblers, Woman with a Fan.*

1906 *Arcady.* Gósol: *The Harem, The Toilette, Three Nudes.* Paris: *Portrait of Gertrude Stein.*

1907 Spring: *Les Demoiselles d'Avignon.* "Primitive" expressionism and pre-Cubism.

1908 Cubism. Sojourn in Rue des Bois.

1909 Summer: Horta de Ebro. Geometric Cubism: *Portrait of Fernande.* Paris: *Portrait of Vollard.*

1910 *Portrait of Uhde, Portrait of Kahnweiler.* Summer in Cadaqués. Abstract Cubism: *The Guitarist.*

1911 Baroque Cubism. Summer in Ceret. Autumn: breaks with Fernande.

1912 First collage: *Still Life with Chair Caning.* Spring-summer: Ceret and Sorgues.

1913 Beginning of the relationship with Eva. *Ma jolie. Jolie Eva.* Ceret (collage). Autumn: *Woman in an Armchair.*

1914 Sojourn in Avignon, with Braque and Derain. Returns to Paris, when war is declared. Pointilliste Cubism. Flat Cubism.

1916. Beginning of his friendship with Cocteau. Realist portraits of Vollard and Max Jacob. Death of Eva.

1917 Visits Italy with Cocteau. Paris: first performance of the ballet *Parade*. Long stay in Barcelona: *The Barcelona Harlequin*.

1918 Marries Olga Koklova.

1919 First representational Cubism: *Table Before the Window*, at Saint-Raphäel.

1921 Second representational Cubism: *Three Musicians*. Sojourn at Fontainebleau. Birth of his son Paulo. Neoclassicism and Gigantism. *Women at the Spring*. Maternities.

1924 Aestheticist cubism: large still lifes.

1925 *The Dance*.

1927 Beginning of the relationship with Marie-Thérèse. Etchings to illustrate Balzac's *Le chef-d'œuvre inconnu*.

1928 Painted visceral sculptures. Abstract sculptures. Summer: Dionysia paroxysm of Dinard.

1932 Curvism: *The Dream*. Figurative sculptures: *Head of Marie-Thérèse*.

1933 *The Sculptor's Studio*, etchings for the "Suite Vollard".

1935 *Minotauromachy* (etching). Birth of Maia.

1936 Beginning of the relationship with Dora Maar.

1937 *Guernica*.

1938 *Woman with Cock*.

1939 *Night Fishing at Antibes*. Autumn: Misshapen or distorted figures from Royan. Self-portraits.

1940 Monsters: *Nude Dressing Her Hair*.

1941-1943 Misshapen or distorted figures in Paris: *Woman in an Armchair*.

1944 *Aubade*. Sculptures: *Death's-head. Man with Sheep*.

1946 Antibes, with Françoise Gilot. *Woman-flower. The Joy of Living*. Ceramics at Vallauris. Series of lithographs.

1947 Birth of Claude.

1949 Birth of Paloma. Peace Congress. Prolific creative activity: ceramics, drawings, paintings, engravings.

1950 Sculptures made with rubbish; *The Goat, The Monkey (1952)*.

1951 Beginning of the relationship with Geneviève Laporte.

1952 *War and Peace*. Lithographic series on Balzac.

1954 Portraits of Sylvette. First appearance of Jacqueline. *Women of Algiers*.

1955-1956 The *Studio in Cannes* series.

1957 *Tauromachy* (aquatints). *The Maids of Honour*.

1958-1960 First series of linocuts.

1959 *The Village of Vauvenargues*.

1960-1961 *The Luncheons*.

1961-1962 Second series of linocuts.

1963 *The Painter and His Model*. Opening of the Picasso Museum in Barcelona.

1966 Great exhibition of homage to Picasso in Paris.

1967 Erotic and burlesque drawings.

1968 The *Suite Crommelinck*: 347 engravings.

1970 *Characters*, exhibited at the Palace of the Popes in Avignon.

1971 Several vividly coloured drawings.

1972 The second *Suite Crommelinck*. A new series of *Characters*.

1973 April 8: death of Picasso at Notre-Dame-de-Vie (Mougins). On April 10 he is buried at Vauvenargues. May 23: opening of a great exhibition of *Characters*, shown for the first time, in the Palace of the Popes in Avignon.

A PRECOCIOUS MASTERY

From his first steps in art, Picasso revealed an extraordinary technical facility, no doubt nurtured by his father, a painter and drawing teacher. While living in La Coruña between 1891 and 1895, the future artist began to take classes in the fine arts, studies that he continued at the School of Fine Arts (known as La Llotja) in Barcelona. From those early years there exist several works in a naturalistic, academic style that attest to Picasso's virtuosity in adolescence. Portraits, some landscapes, and social themes of a compassionate nature—which reappear in the Blue Period—are the typical genres during this period. The influence of Muñoz Degrain, a nineteenth-century painter highly esteemed by Picasso's father, is perhaps the most evident. The honorable mention of the young artist's work *Science and Charity* at the National Exhibition of Fine Arts in 1897, closes this chapter of Picasso's development as an academic painter. What would have been an excellent start to the career of a conventional painter of the period was for Picasso the last stage before pursuing a very different course.

THE FARM AT QUIQUET, 1898. Painted one year after *Science and Charity,* this work reflects a different, happier spirit, far from the dark palette characteristic of academic painting.

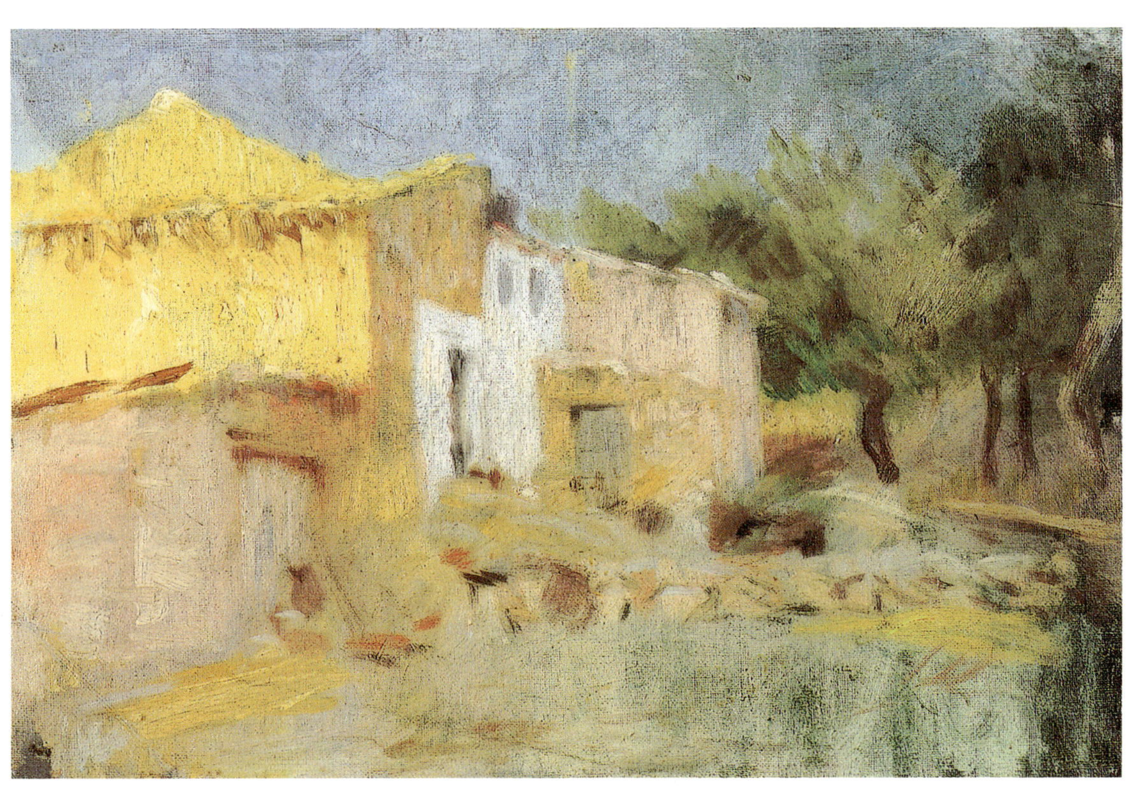

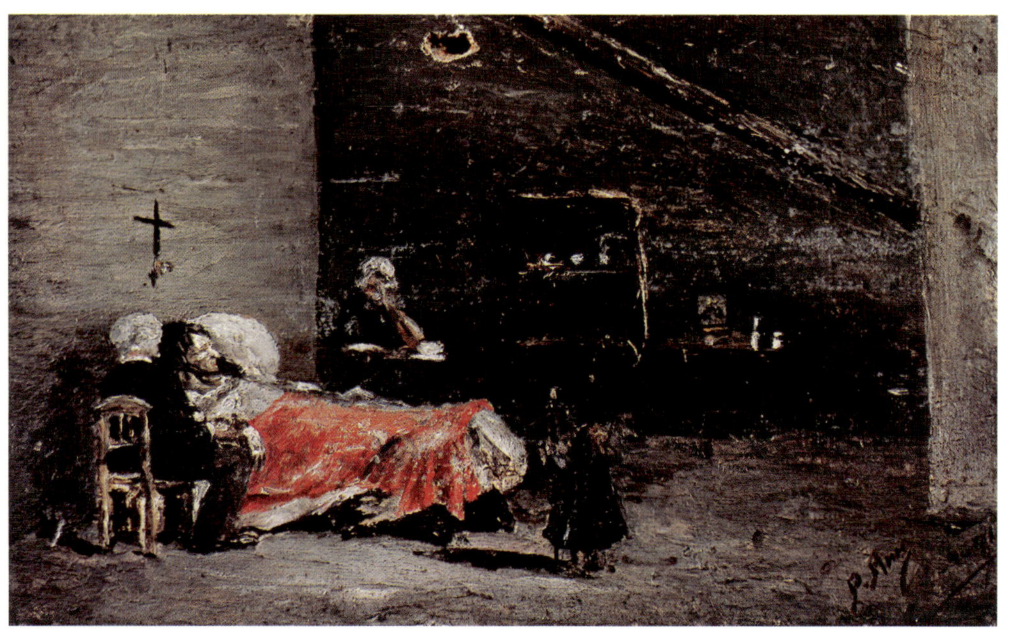

THE SICK WOMAN, 1894. The
illness that caused the death
of Picasso's sister Concepción
appears to have signaled a dark
period for Picasso, tinged with
death and grief. This small
canvas, painted when he was
still in La Coruña, foreshadows
the compassionate treatment
of such themes that culminated
three years later
in *Science and Charity*.

SCIENCE AND CHARITY, 1897.
Science is personified by the
doctor taking the pulse of the
patient, whose hand already has
the ashen pallor of death.
Charity is personified
by a nun who tends to the child
as she offers a drink to the
sick woman. Picasso began and
ended his career in academic
painting with this canvas, for
which his father and his sister
Lola posed, and which reveals
an in expertise unusual in a
sixteen-year-old.

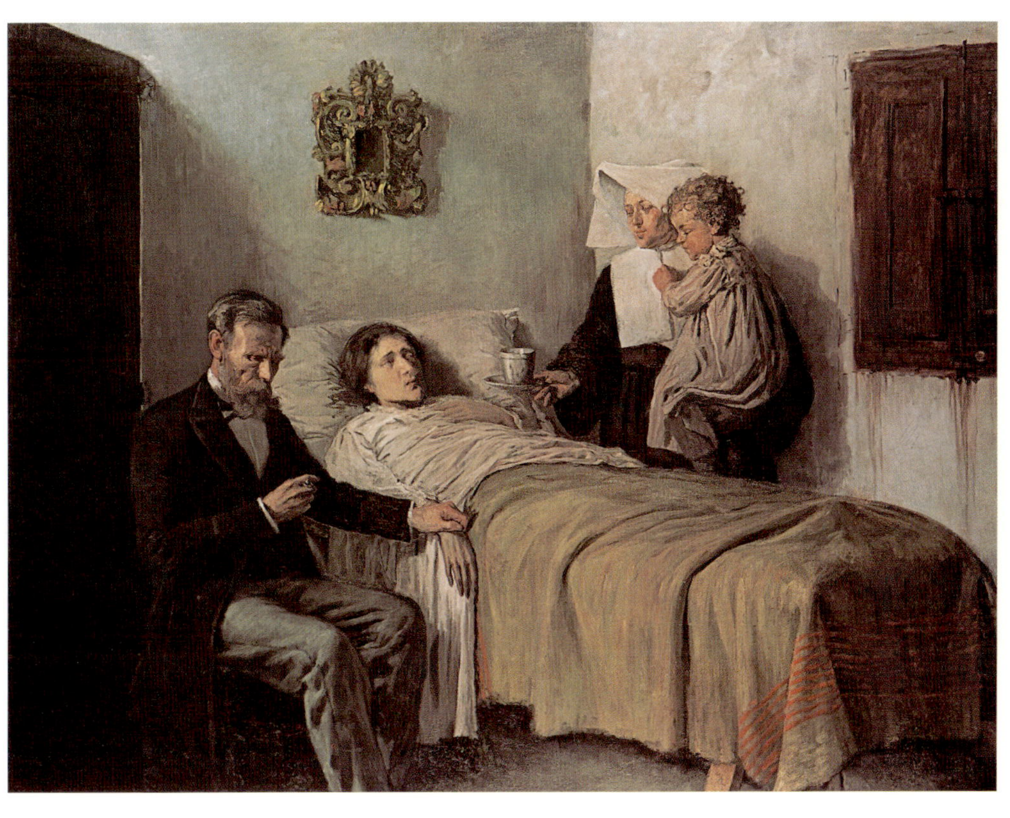

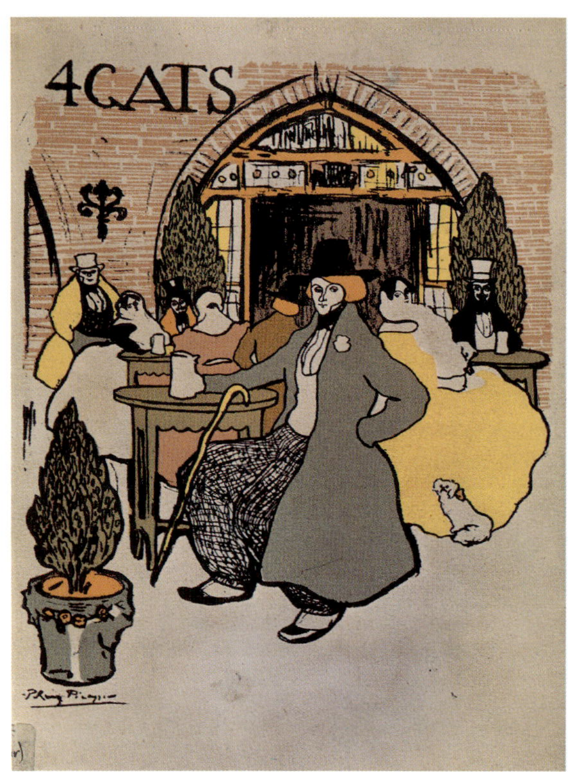

BARCELONA, FIN-DE-SIÈCLE

Picasso had his first studio at no. 4 carrer de la Plata, in Barcelona. The multiple stimuli offered to him by the city, at that time very much a part of the European art scene, soon led him to a Bohemian lifestyle that he shared with other young artists. He would meet with his first circle of friends—among them Carles Casagemas, Manuel Pallarès, and Sebastià Junyer Vidal—at Els Quatre Gats tavern. There he met the most important Catalan artists of the time, such as Isidre Nonell, Joaquim Mir, Julio González, and Ramon Pitxot, and it was also there, in 1900, that he held the first exhibition of his works. Until the end of the first decade of the century Picasso maintained strong ties to Barcelona, although beginning in 1904 he was already residing in Paris on a steady basis. Before venturing in his decidedly personal creative direction, Picasso experimented with almost all the stylistic modes offered by the art of his time, from Post-Impressionism and Symbolism to the genre of cafe and brothel scenes in the style of Edgar Degas or Henri de Toulouse-Lautrec.

POSTER FOR THE MENU OF ELS QUATRE GATS, 1900. Pere Romeu, manager of the establishment that best represents the painter's Barcelona period, commissioned this work, which follows the style of "Modernista" poster art predominant in that era.

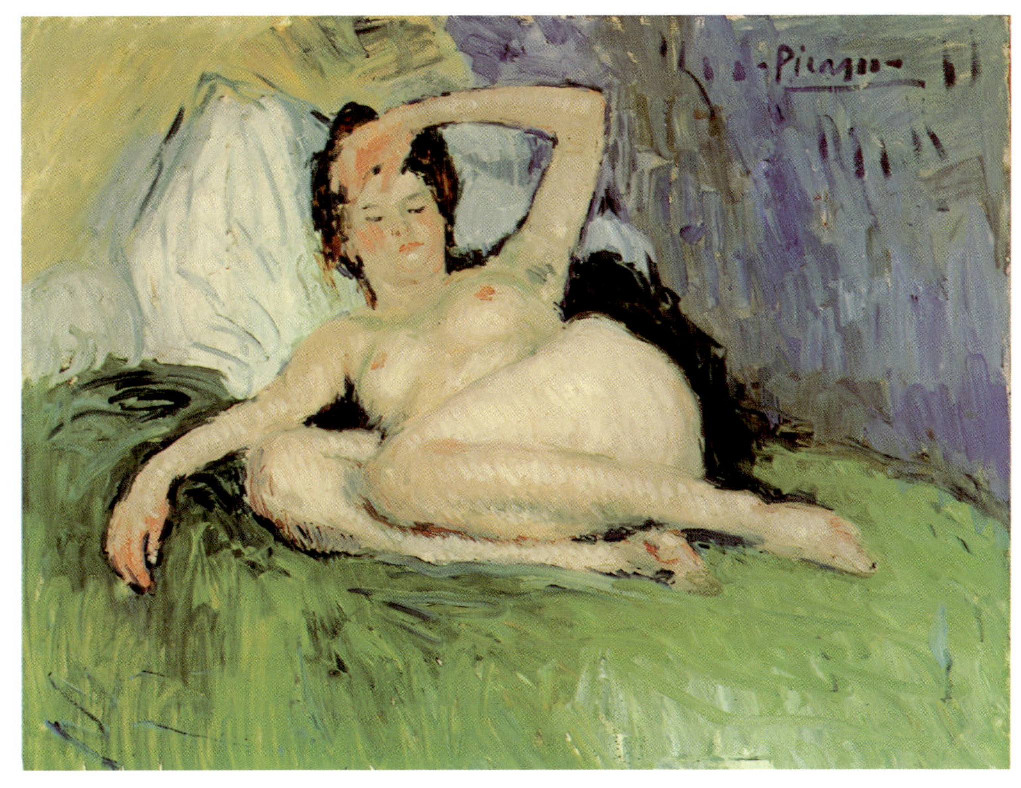

FEMALE NUDE, 1901. A harmony of blue, yellow, and green serves as a background for this nude, painted in Paris, but similar in style to that of the painters who dominated the Catalan artistic scene in those first years of the new century.

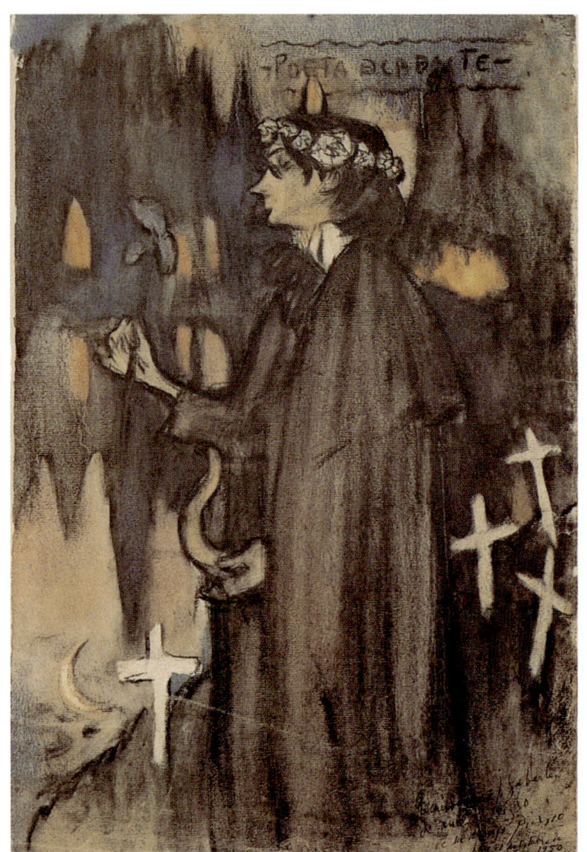

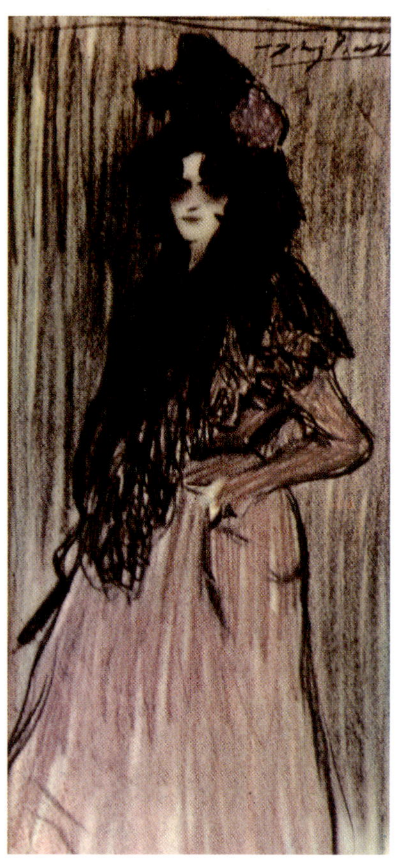

SABARTÉS, "DECADENT POET", 1900.
MANOLA (INSPIRED BY LOLA RUIZ
PICASSO), 1900. The subjects—
Picasso's friend Sabartés and
his sister Lola—belonged to the
immediate circle of the painter.
The Symbolist treatment of these
figures reflects the cultural
fashion of the time. Both
canvases formed part of the
exhibition in 1900 at Els
Quatre Gats.

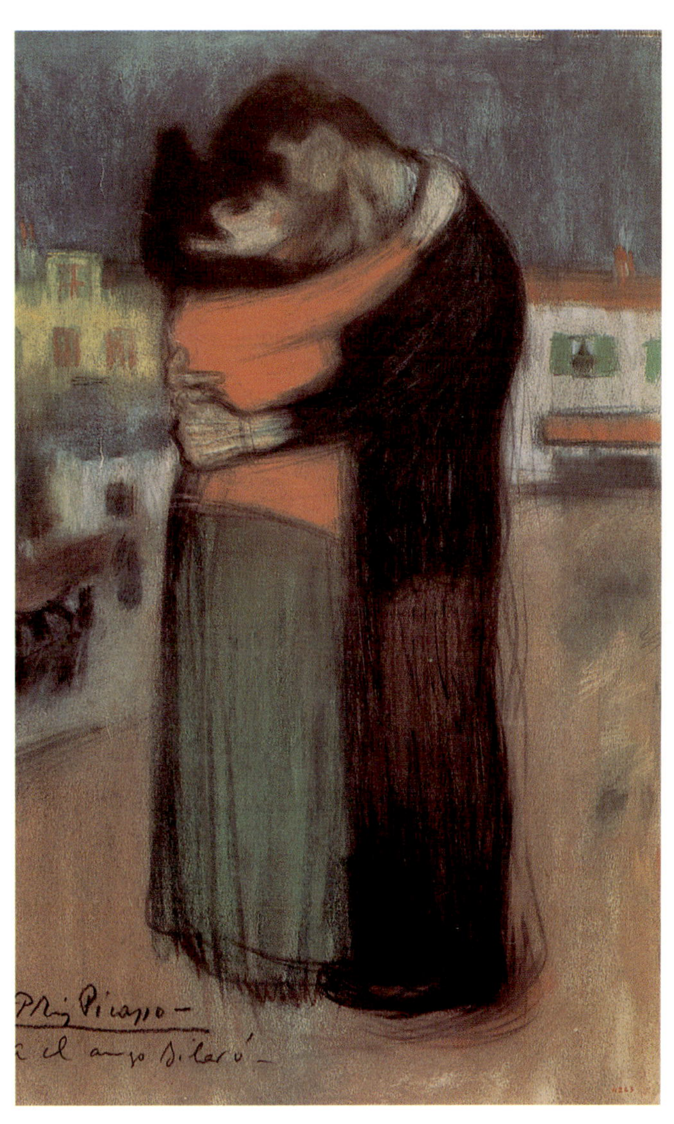

STREET EMBRACE, 1900.
The firmness of the pictorial
gesture, the rotundity of
the figures, and the somber
atmosphere of the scene clearly
evoke the influence of Isidro
Nonell, in whose Paris studio
Picasso and Carles Casagemas
stayed during their trip that
same year.

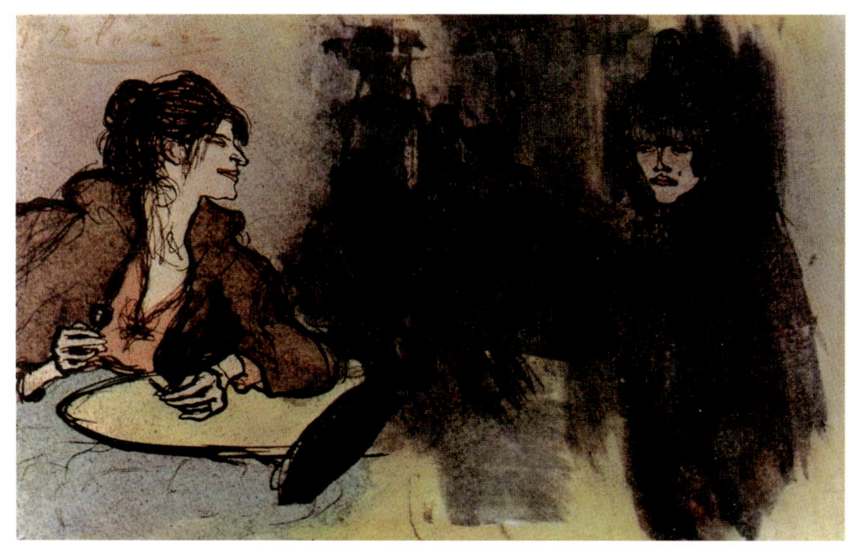

TWO FEMALE FIGURES, 1900. The
great precision and fluidity
of the drawing and the depiction
of Bohemian life and nighttime
revelry recall Edgar Degas and
Henri de Toulouse-Lautrec, both
especially fond of this type of
rapid exercise in watercolor.

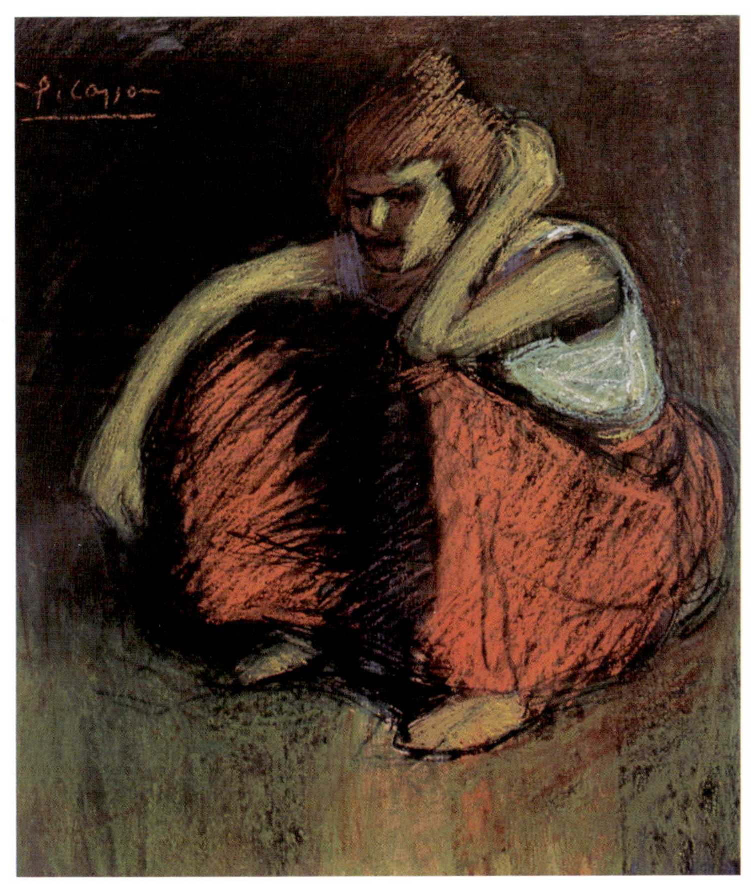

THE RED SKIRT, 1901. This
pastel likewise recalls
Toulouse-Lautrec and Degas,
but with a greater chromatic
violence and, above all,
a characteristic interest
in the volume of the figure.

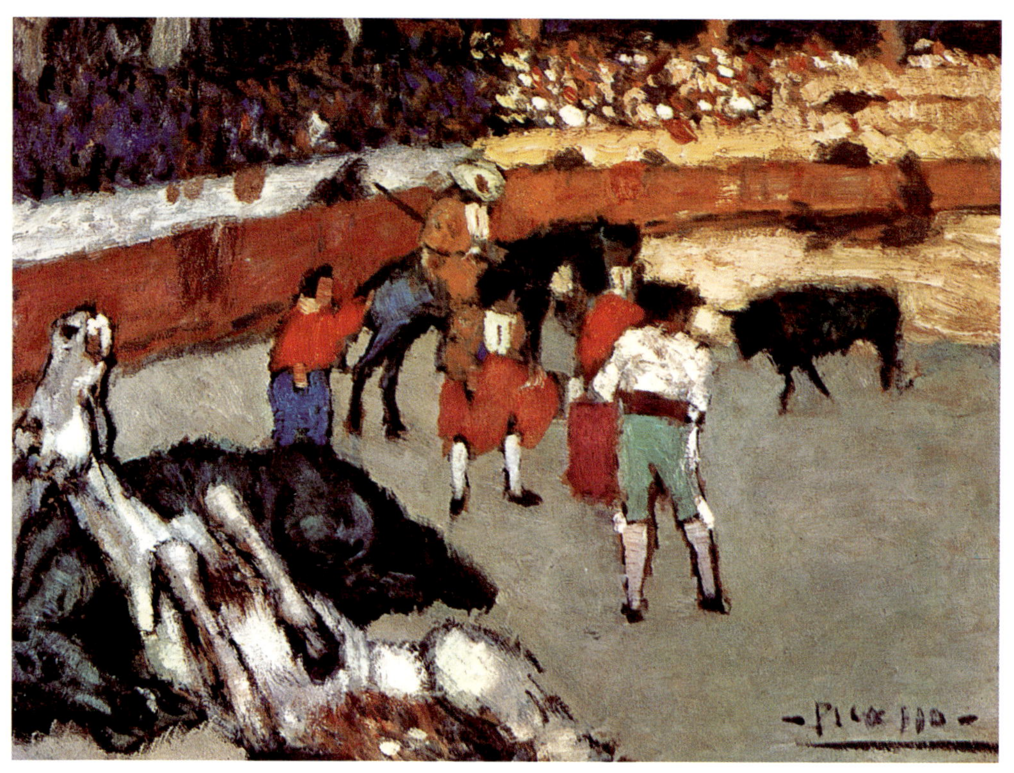

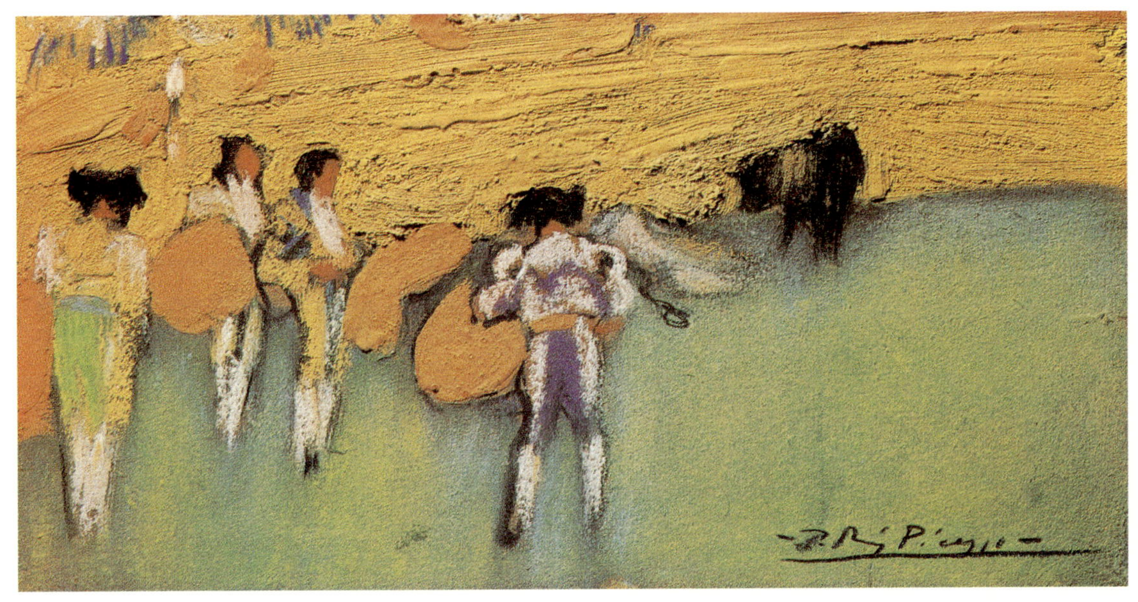

BULLFIGHT SCENE, 1901. BULLFIGHTERS AND BULL IN ANTICIPATION, 1900.
Picasso, a true aficionado of the bullfight, painted several
bullfighting scenes in the early part of his career. He would
not return to the subject matter until many years later, when
it became a vehicle for his personal mythology.

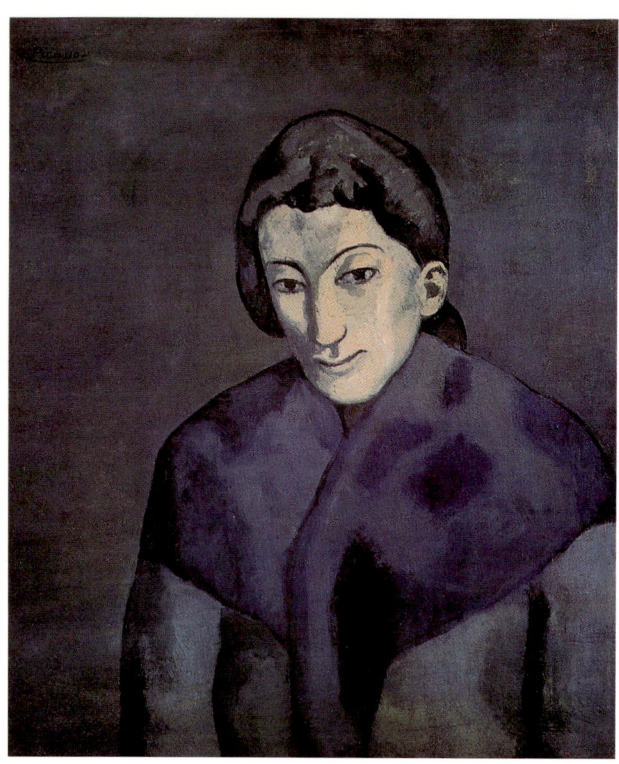

BLUE AND ROSE PERIODS

Between 1900 and 1906, coinciding with his initial immersion in the French artistic scene, Picasso began the first truly personal phase of his career. The influence of "modernista" Barcelona is still apparent in some of the canvases of this period, revealing a decadent, Symbolist inspiration in harmony with fin-de-siècle taste. Figures of monumental bearing stand out against monochrome backgrounds in which the color blue or rose predominates, thus giving a label to the work of these periods. It is difficult to establish a division between the Blue Period and the Rose Period, although in the former moody and melancholic subject matter is more in evidence: beggars, mothers and children cast in apparent poverty, decrepit old age and inner sadness populate these canvases. In them one can perceive the influence of Isidro Nonell and El Greco, whose painting was starting to be in vogue at the beginning of this century. In the Rose Period, however, there is a frequent appearance of fairground performers and circus figures, characters the Montmartre painters were very fond of depicting. Still very young, Picasso sketched out a new path which he was capable of exploring with assured ease before abandoning it to leap once again into the unknown.

WOMAN WITH A SCARF, 1902. One of the first examples of the so-called Blue Period; nonetheless the work reveals a capcity for synthesis in the depiction of the figure, that foreshadows the paintings that gave rise to Cubism four years later.

BOY WITH DOG, 1905. The flat, linear treatment of the subject bears witness to the influence of Catalan "modernisme" that Picasso was then starting to leave behind.

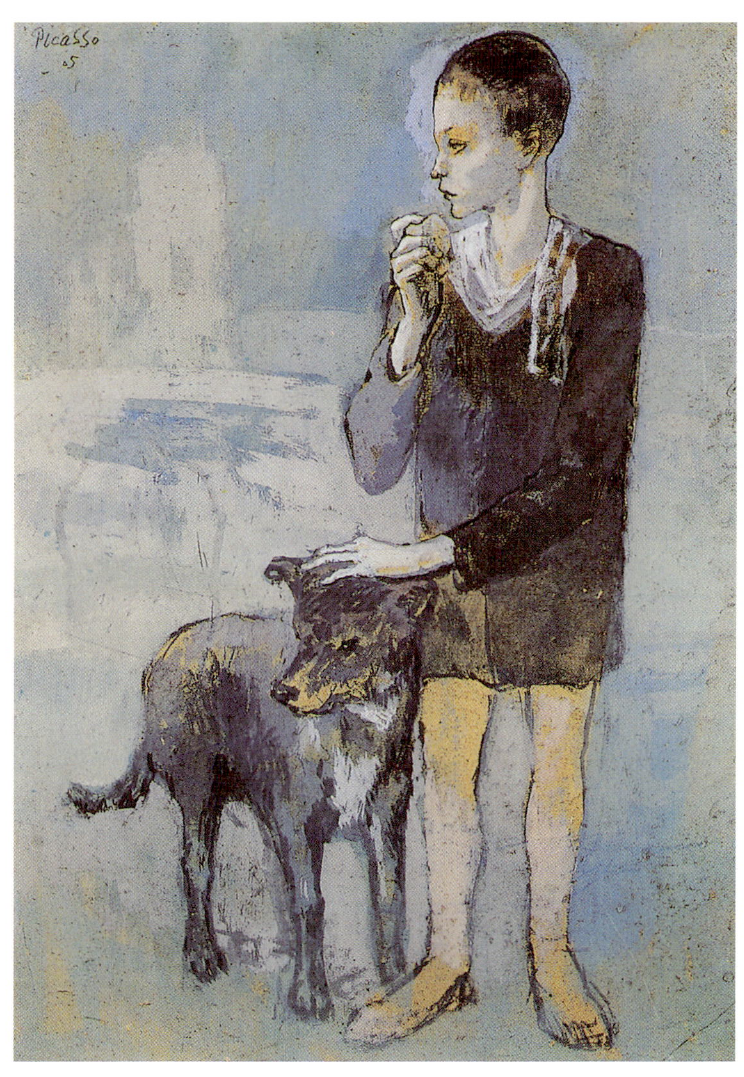

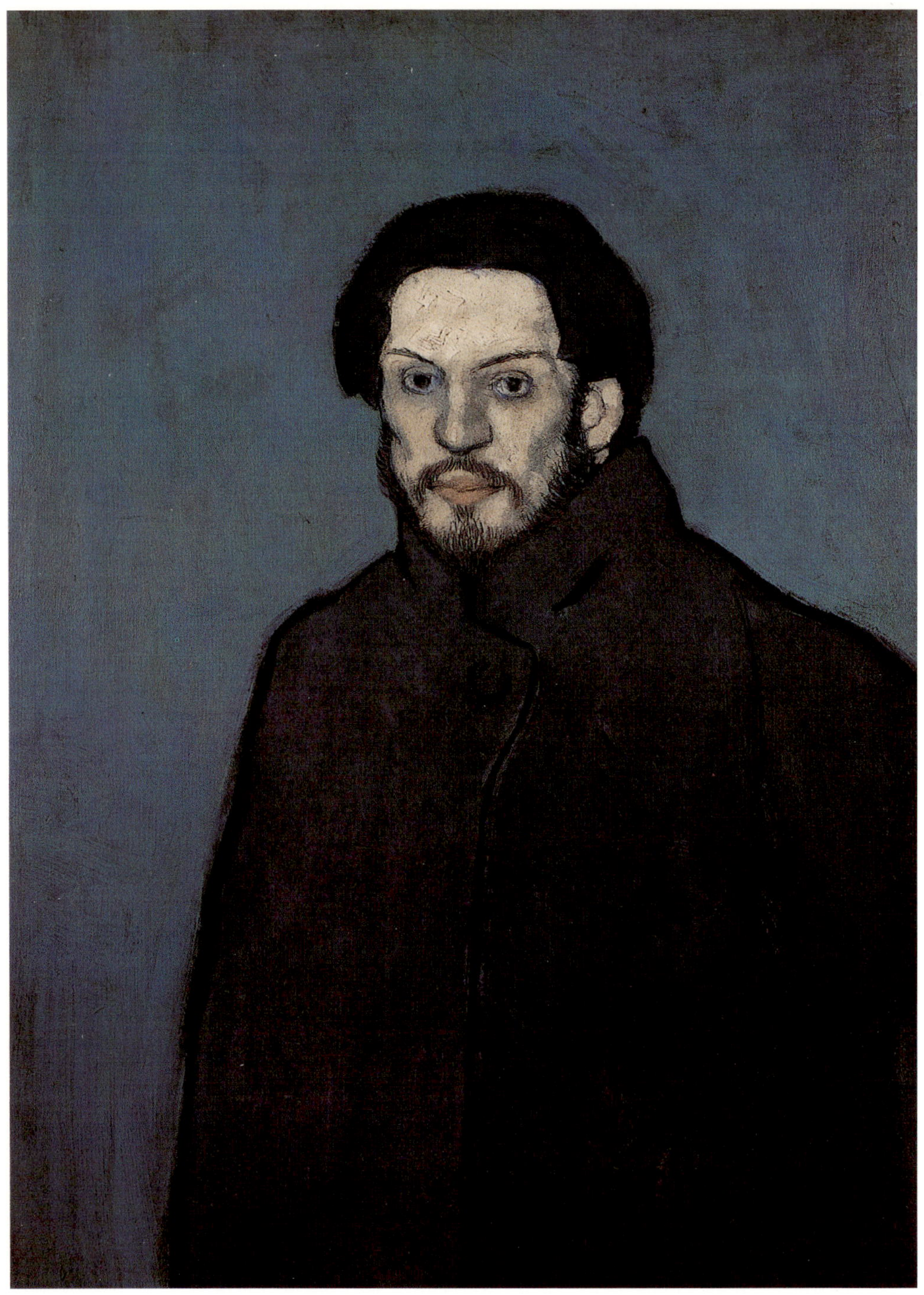

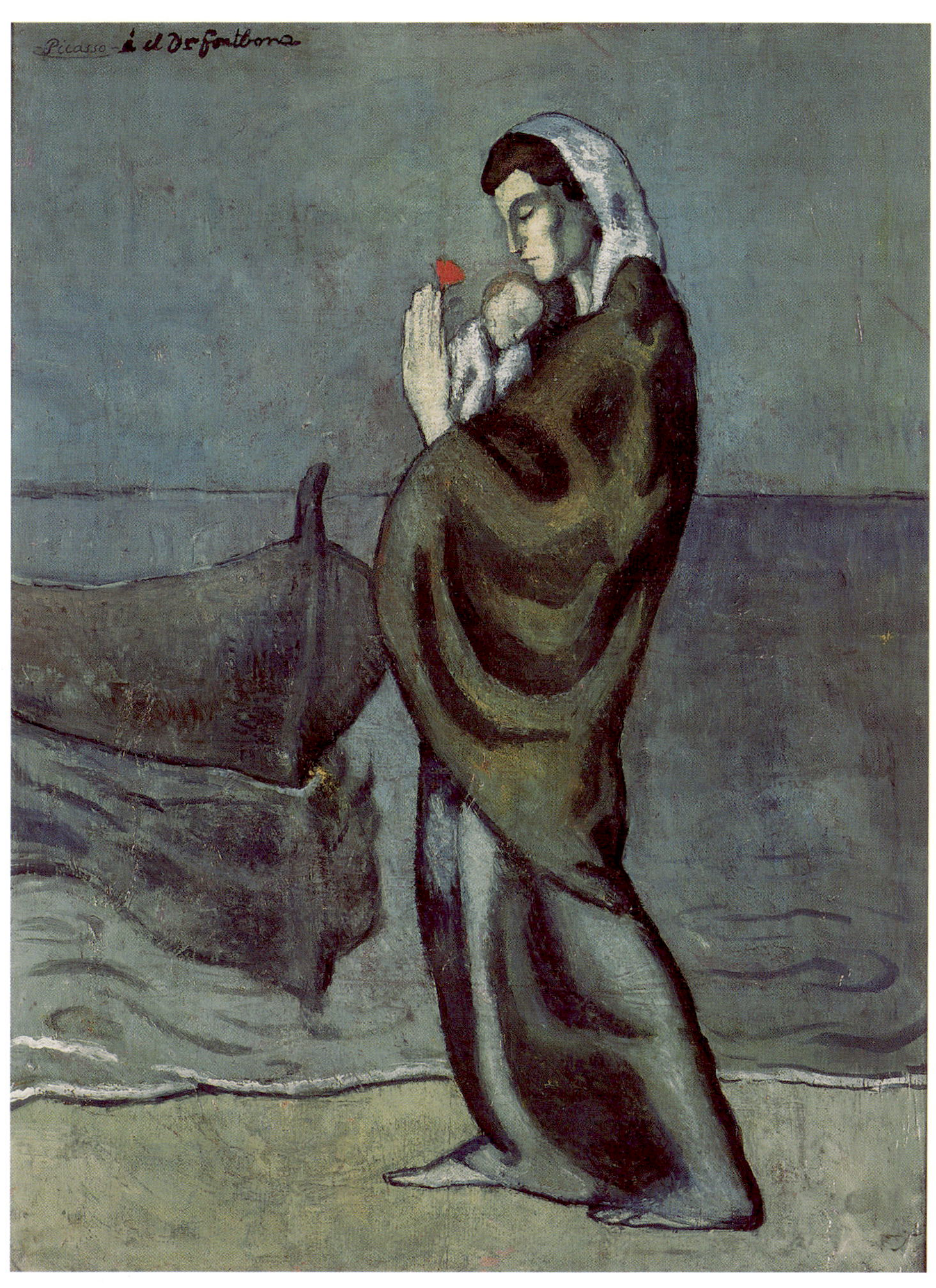

SELF-PORTRAIT, 1901. Realized with a great economy of means,
this is one of many self-portraits that the painter would complete
throughout his career. The traits of depression and premature aging,
surprising in a man barely twenty, reflect the melancholy and
pessimism associated with fin-de-siècle culture.

MATERNITY BESIDE THE SEA, 1902. The allegory implicit in the
subject is characteristic of fin-de-siecle Symbolism, a movement
that was firmly rooted in Barcelona in those years.

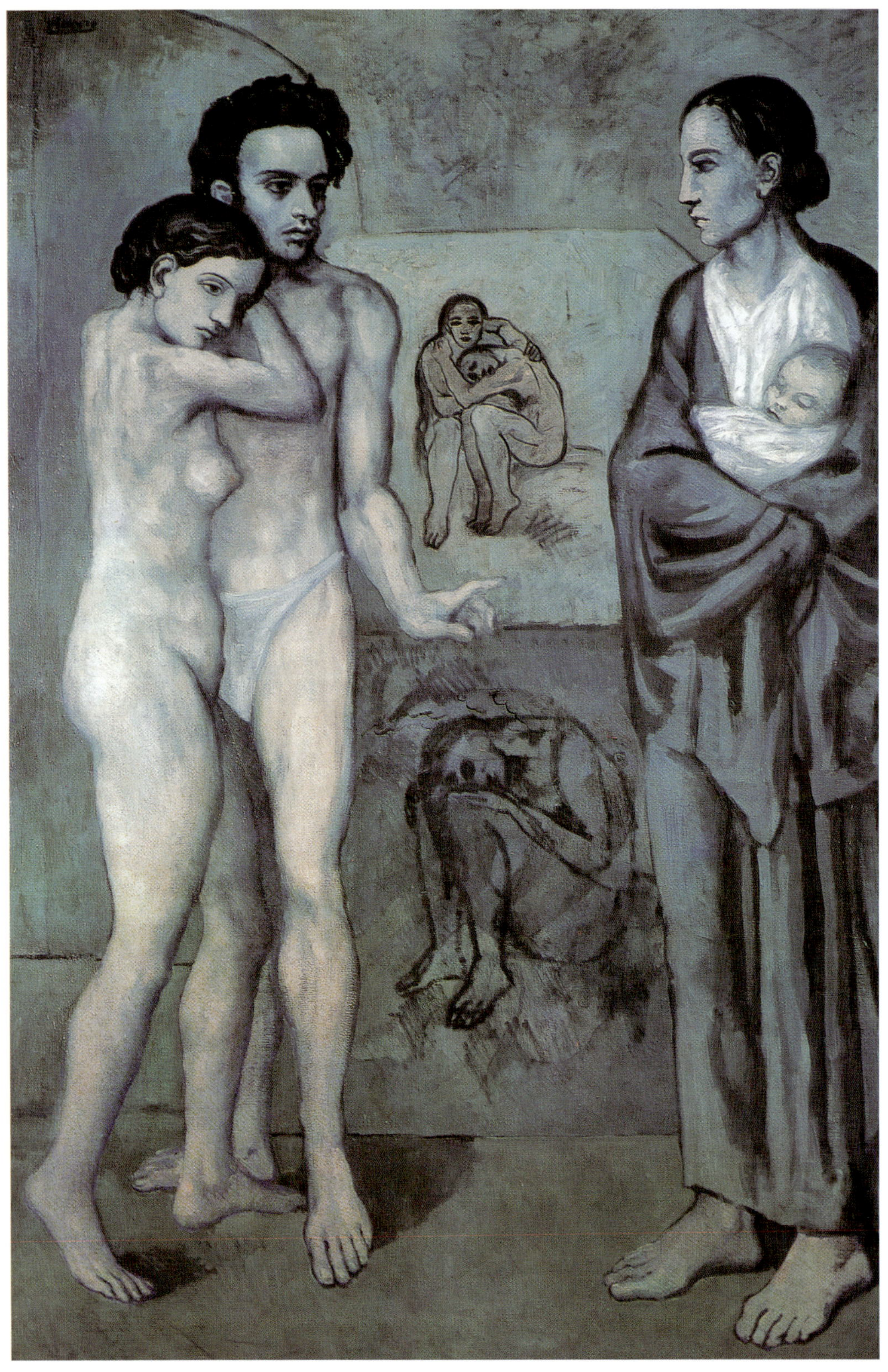

LA VIE, 1902. This large-scale
allegory was the most ambitious
canvas undertaken by Picasso
until that time. Conceived as
a group of symbolic figures
with open-ended significance,
it is atribute to his friend
Carles Casagemas—the
male seminude figure—who had
committed suicide in Paris
the previous year, following
a failed romance.

THE MADMAN, 1904. Like many
canvases of the period, this
small watercolor on wrapping
paper is dedicated to Picasso's
friend Sebastià Junyer Vidal and
reveals the command of drawing
of which Picasso was always
proud.

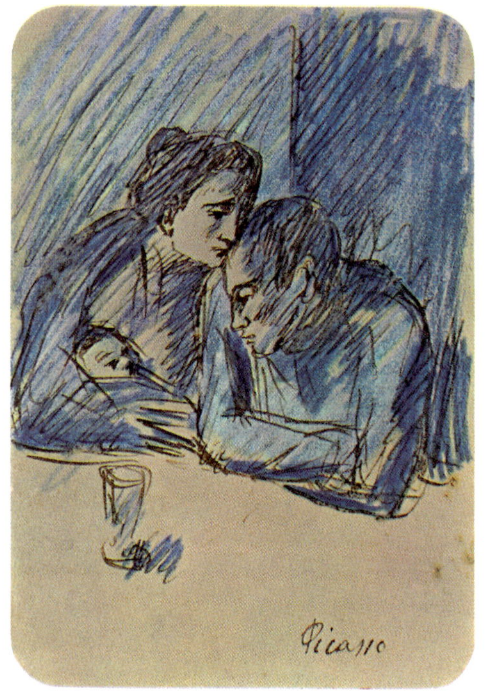

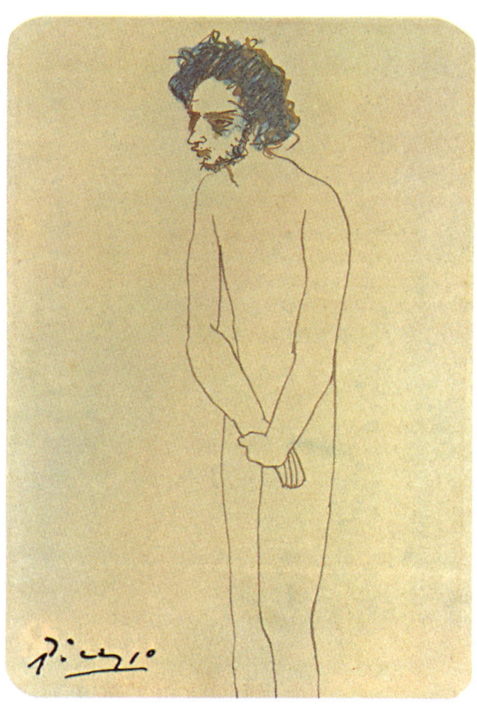

COUPLE WITH CHILD AT THE CAFE,
1903. CASAGEMAS NUDE, 1904. From
the Bohemian years in Barcelona
and Paris at the beginning of
the century there still exist
many of these small drawings
that share the desolate quality
of Picasso's contemporaneous
paintings.

MEDITATION (CONTEMPLATION), 1904.
One of the first paintings
Picasso completed in Paris
after taking up residence at
the Bateau-Lavoir in Montmartre.
Despite the warm atmosphere
of the ochre and reddish
tones, this studio scene,
which includes a self-portrait,
does not completely abandon
the pathos of Picasso's works
of those years.

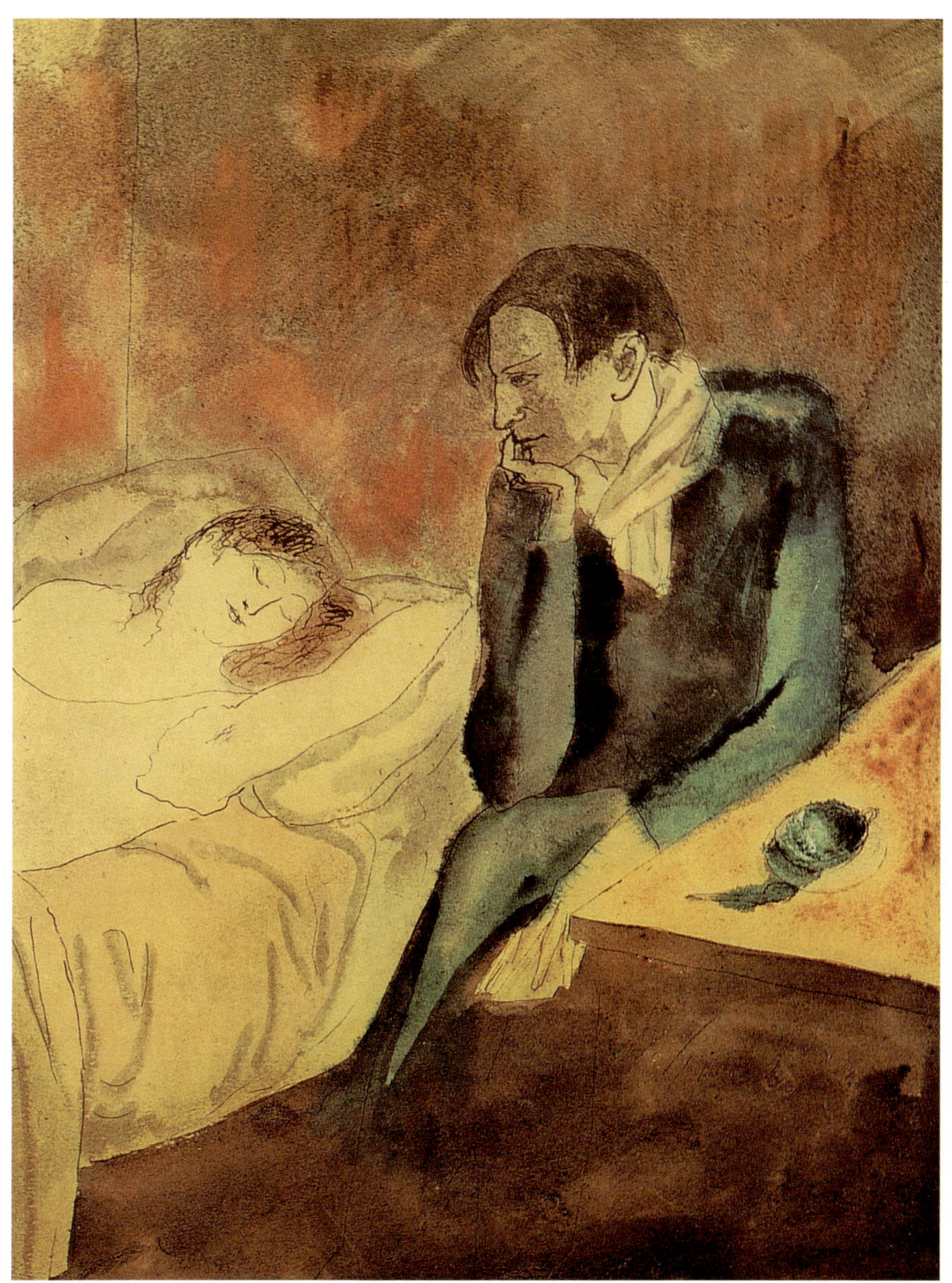

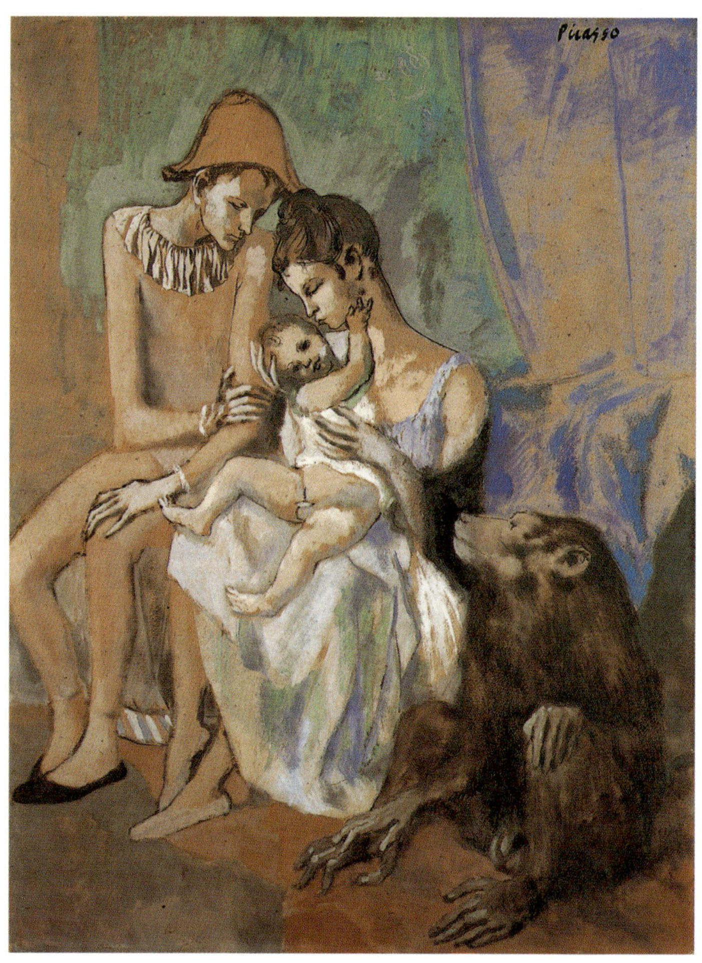

THE ACROBAT'S FAMILY WITH A MONKEY, 1905. A backstage circus scene characteristic of the so-called Rose Period. The placement of the figures in a plane that is near but oblique to that of the canvas is a typical device of painters such as Edgar Degas and Edouard Manet, who so interested Picasso in that period. The shallow treatment in the depiction of space avoids illusionistic excess.

ACROBAT ON A BALL, 1905. This is one of the first canvases in which one clearly perceives Picasso's interest in the portrayal of mass. While the balancer has the flat, decorative planarity of Picasso's figures of that period, the large figure in the foreground is modeled with a marked chiaroscuro technique.

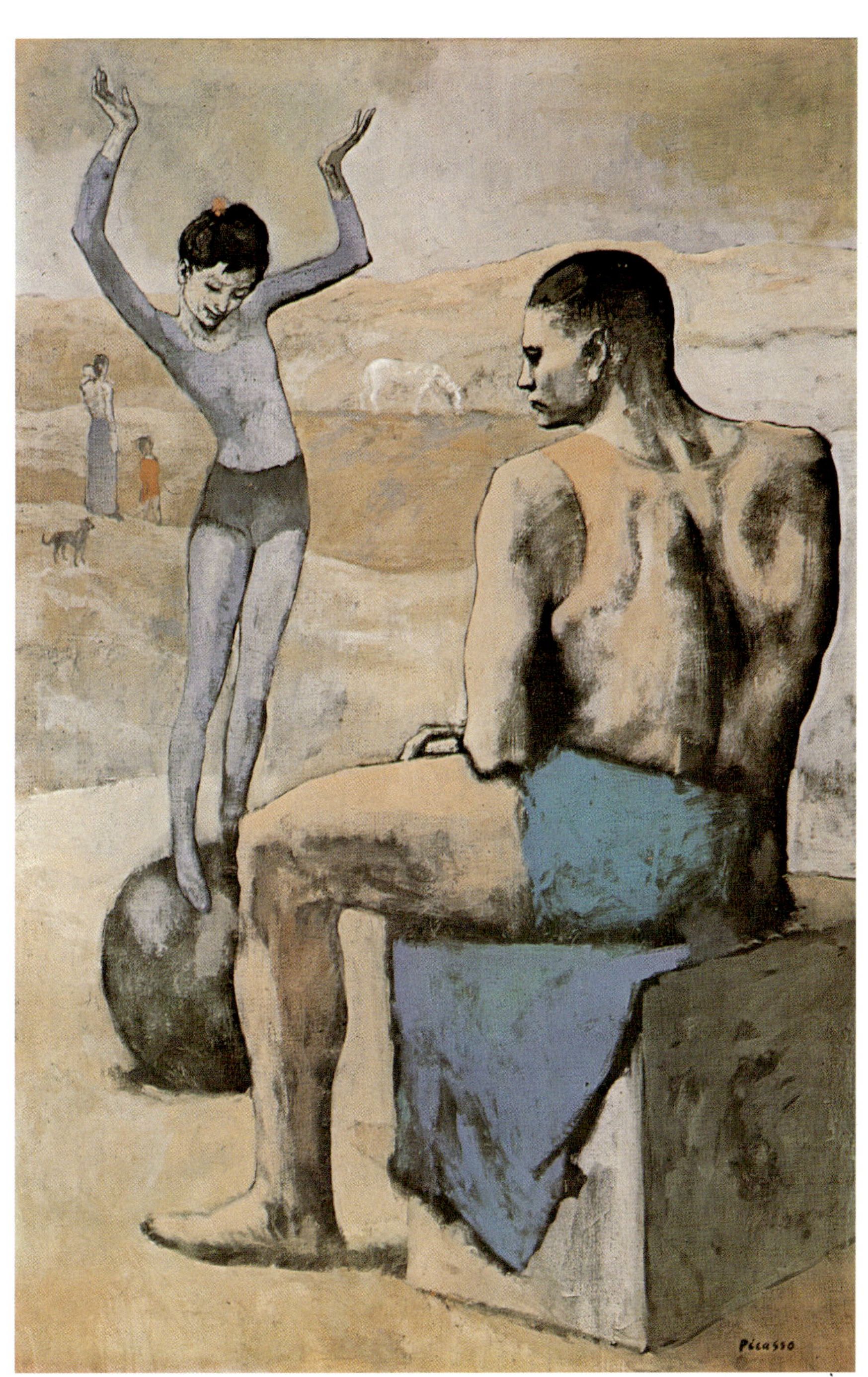

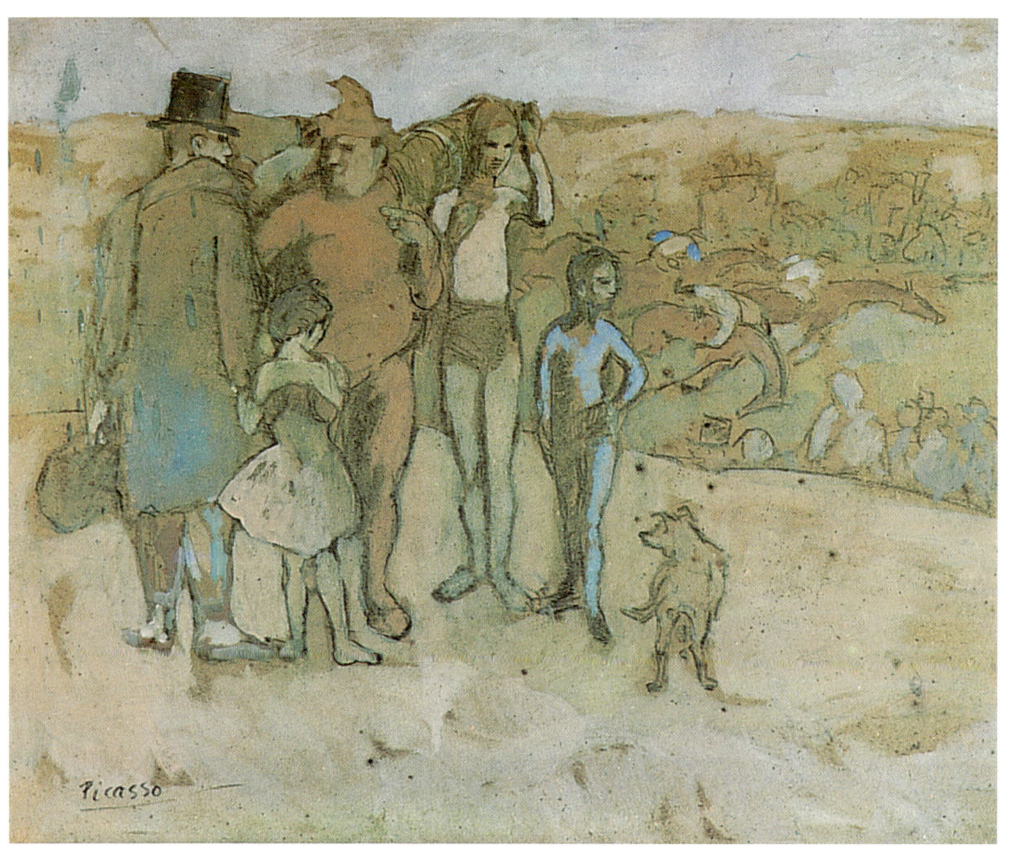

FAMILY OF ACROBATS, 1905. Circus
performers often appear in the
work of the Montmartre painters
of the period who empathized
with the subjects' marginal
place in society and were
attracted to the pictorial
possibilities they offered.

LA TOILETTE, 1906. Picasso
painted this canvas in Gósol,
located in the Pyrenees
near the city of Lleida.
It represents one of the last
works faithful to the fin-de-
siècle style. That same autumn
the painter would begin studies
for *Les Demoiselles d'Avignon*.

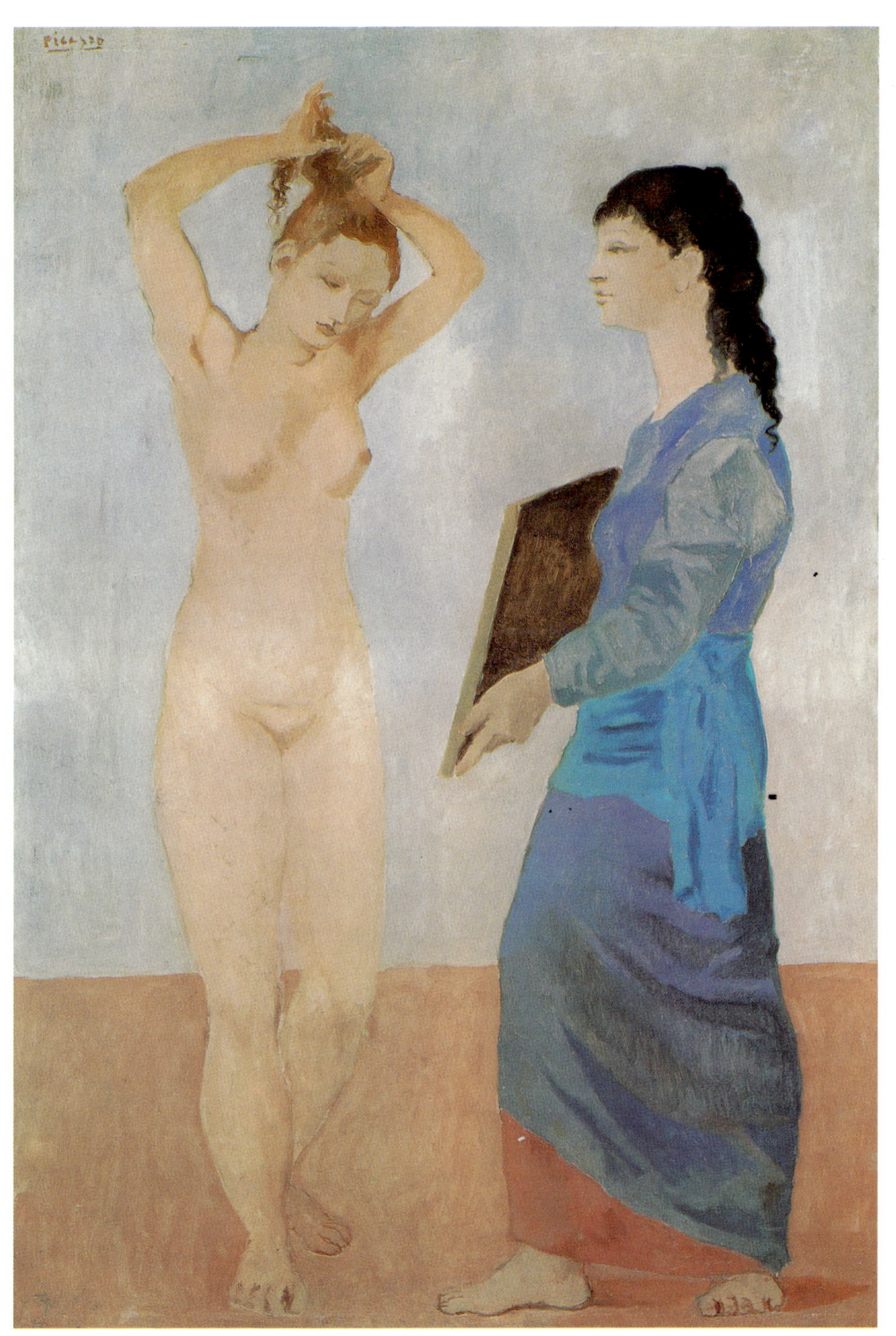

THE THRESHOLD OF CUBISM

Already in some canvases of the so-called Rose Period, Picasso
had shown interest in expressing the solidity of masses through
the constructive quality of the brushstroke. The presence of the
paintings of Paul Cézanne as the inspiration for that method is quite
apparent. By adding another important influence, the non-imitative
representation of reality that Picasso found in Iberian sculpture, and
particularly in the African statues and masks exhibited in the Musée
du Trocadéro, we have all the elements necessary to understand the
transformation of his work in 1906, which culminated the following
year in the famous painting *Les Demoiselles d'Avignon*. Picasso had
not tackled such a large format previously. Preparatory studies
document the creative process behind this important work, which
was first conceived in a much more naturalistic manner.
Also revealed in the studies was the inclusion of two dressed male
figures, which would have placed the work within the genre of brothel
scenes, although the figures were finally painted out of the canvas.
This revolutionary painting displaced Henri Matisse's work *Le bonheur
de vivre* as the privileged topic of discussion at Gertrude Stein's
regular soirées, which served as the favorite salon of the Parisian
literary and artistic avant-garde of the time. Picasso's painting caused
a profound impression on all those who viewed it, conscious as they
were that the future path of modern painting was prefigured in its
subject matter and style.

PORTRAIT OF GERTRUDE STEIN,
1905-06. Although this was one
of the few times that Picasso
painted a portrait with the
model present, in the end his
tendency toward experimentation
took precedence. The sitter's
face is stylized and masklike,
and the mass of her body is
ambiguously placed within
the space, foreshadowing the
compositional complexity of
Les Demoiselles d'Avignon
one year later.

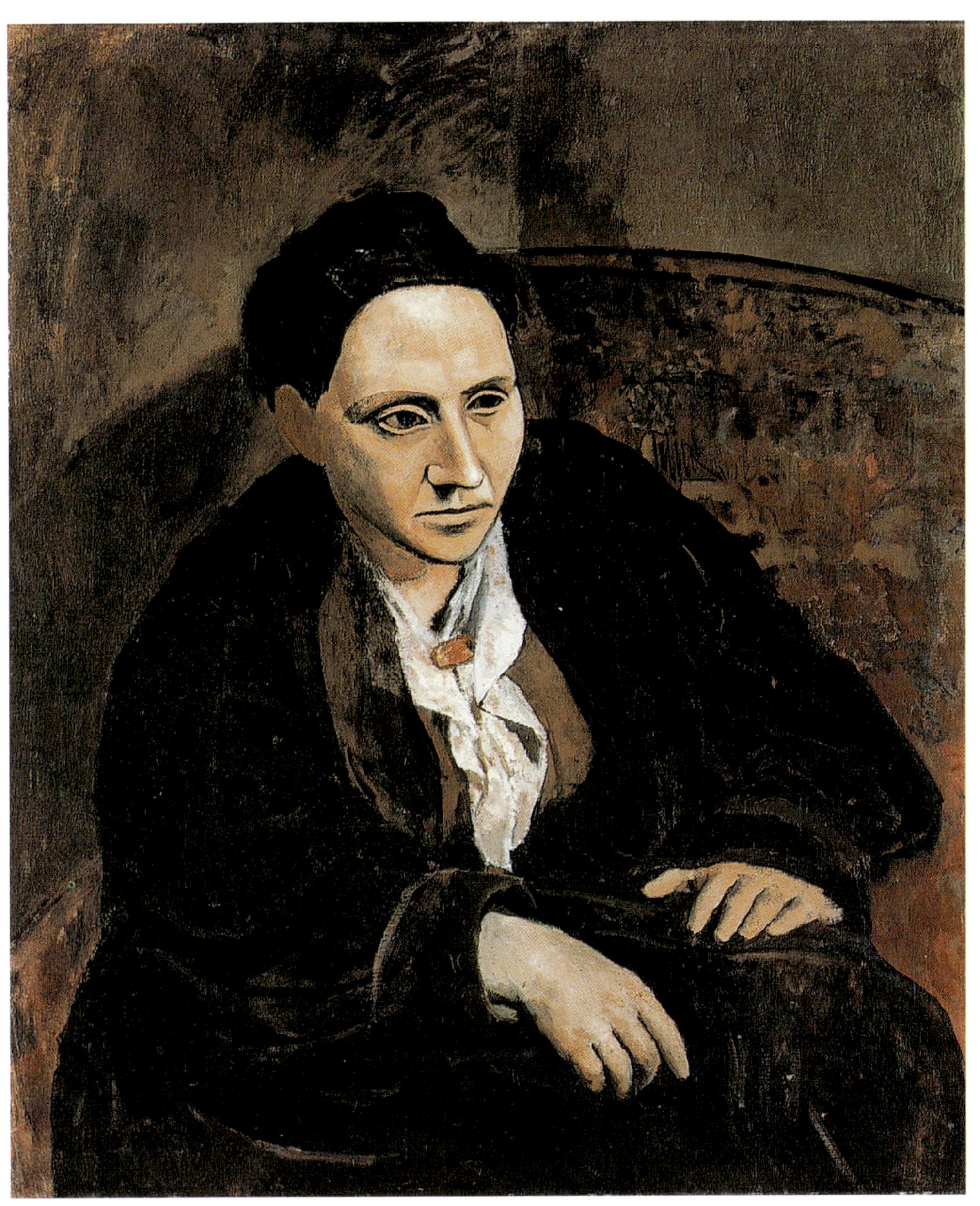

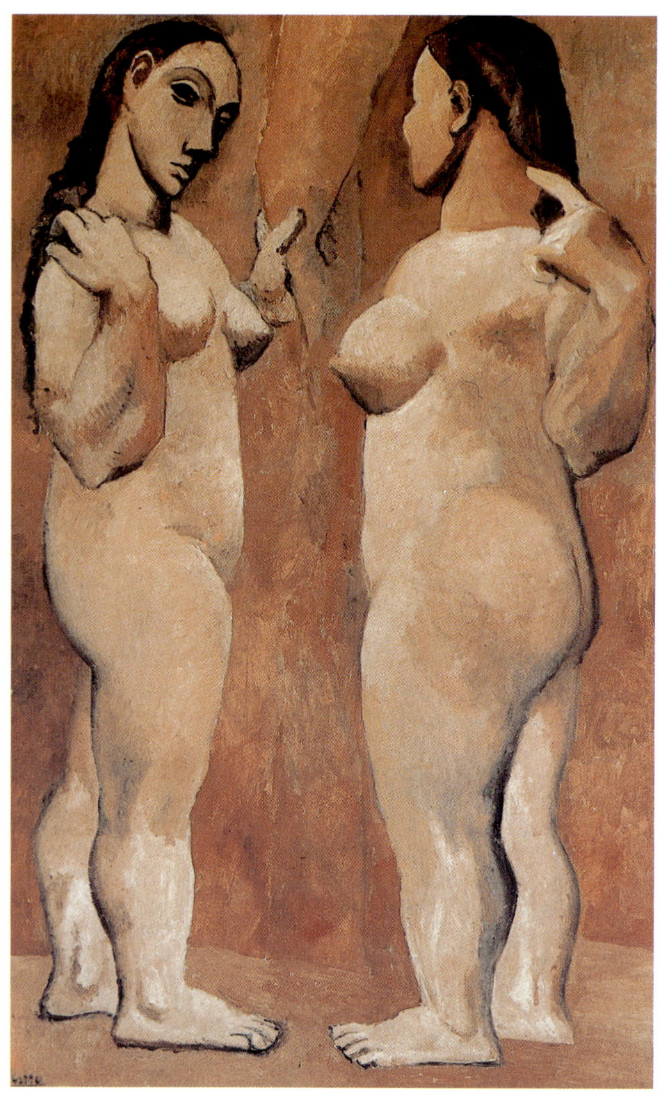

TWO NUDES, 1906. The earth
tones are related to the work
of the Rose Period; however,
Picasso stressed the almost
sculptural mass of the figures,
revealing the inspiration of
Iberian art during those years.
Also suggested by the solidity
of the figures is the artist's
growing interest in the painting
of Paul Cézanne.

LES DEMOISELLES D'AVIGNON, 1907.
The influence of Paul Cezanne's
Bathers is evident in the three
women on the left, although the
forms have been simplified and
the noses on the forward-facing
countenances are depicted in
profile. The two women on
the right and the still life,
however, signal the first
manifestation of Cubism:
the heads are portrayed with
images of African masks,
and the bodies are faceted
in juxtaposed planes, united
with the surrounding space
by a similarity in treatment.

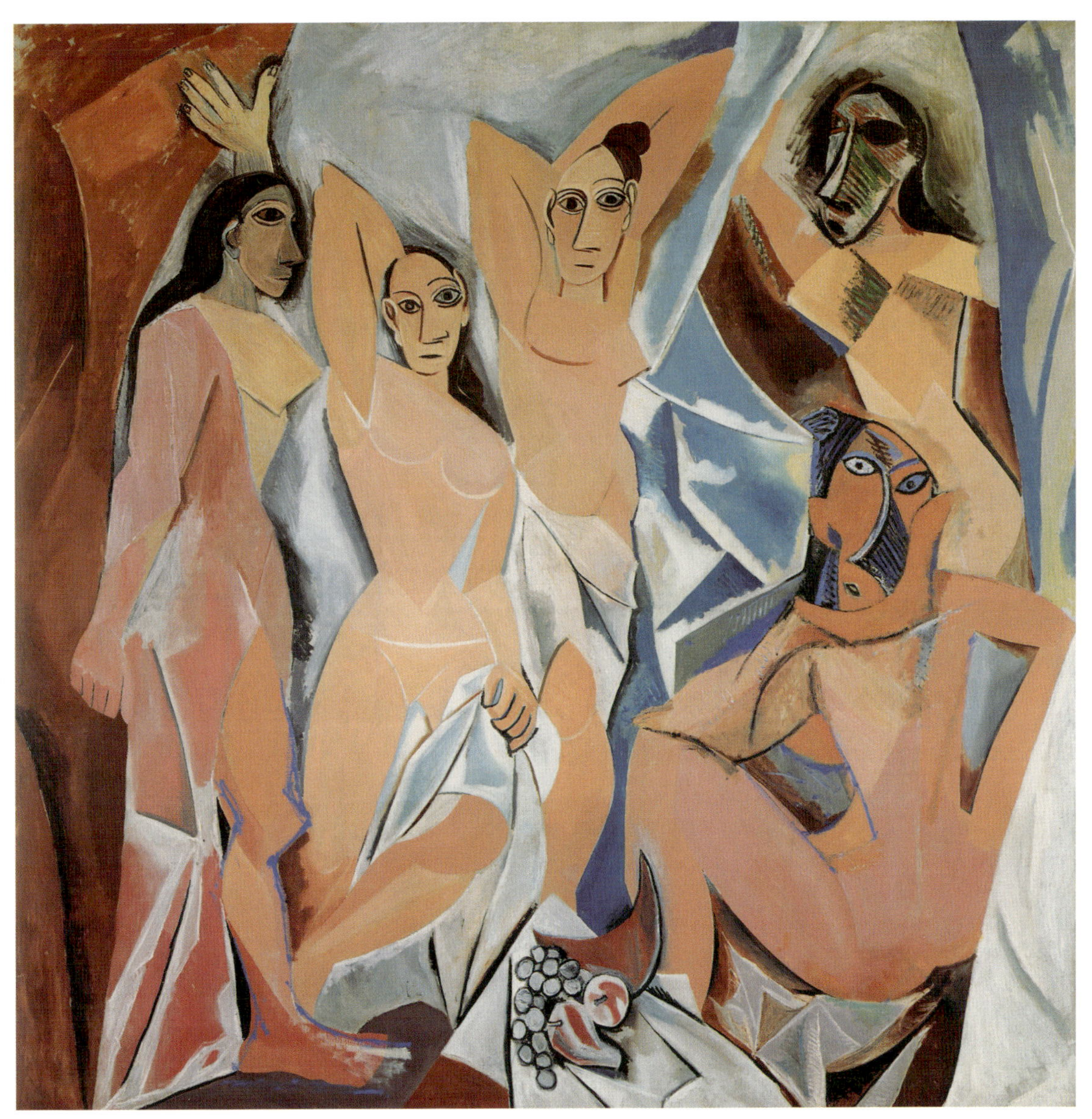

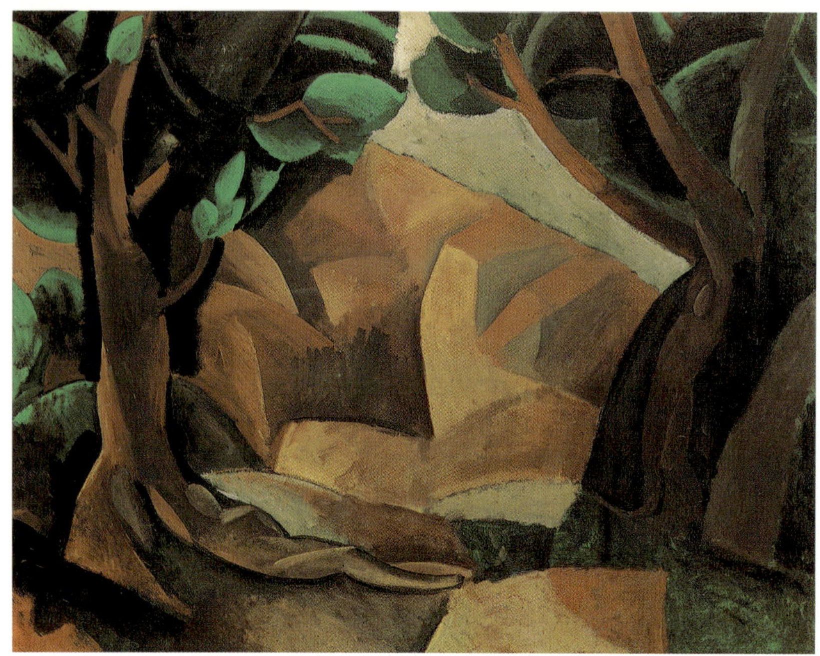

ANALYTICAL CUBISM

The formative stage of Cubism is almost a private affair between Georges Braque and Picasso. Only a small group of friends—nearly all of them writers—such as Guillaume Apollinaire, André Salmon, Max Jacob and D.H. Kahnweiler (whose support as a patron was fundamental to this venture) had access to it, for until 1919 neither protagonist held an individual exhibition. Working "like two mountaineers on the same rope," in Braque's words, they labored intensely to formulate the principles of this new mo de of painting. Picasso's paintings until 1909 continue to reveal a concern for form, and for the profiling and regularizing of masses, as can be seen in the works he painted that summer in Horta de Ebro (now Horta de Sant Joan). Over the next two years his fundamental concern was to integrate the volumes and space of the painting into a single scheme of faceted planes, modulating the pictorial surface as though it were a bas-relief. Following the lesson of Paul Cézanne, the brushstroke acquires a primarily constructive value; hence Picasso's renunciation in this period of the use of color, which contributes to the paintings' possessing that character of hermetic grisailles.

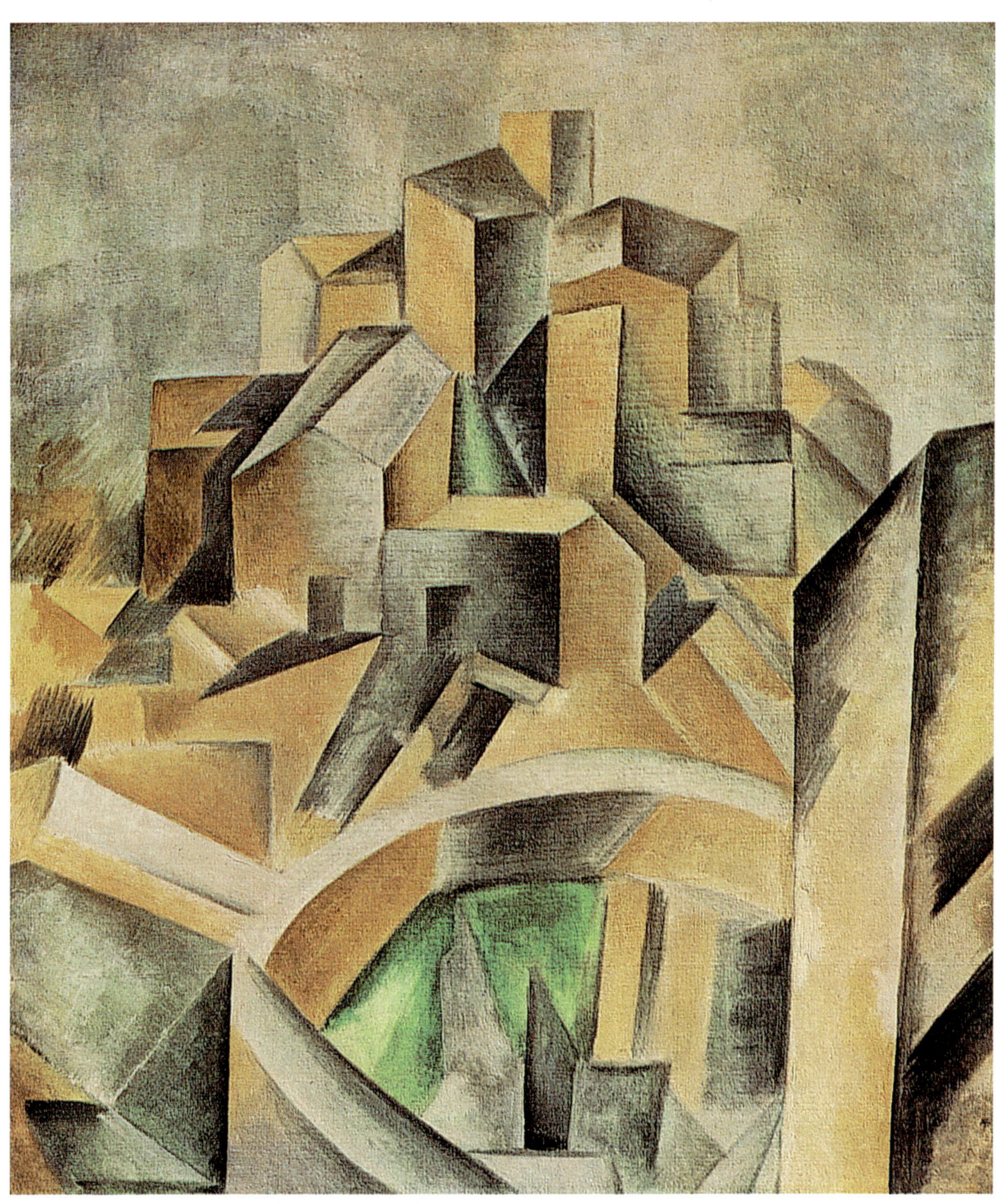

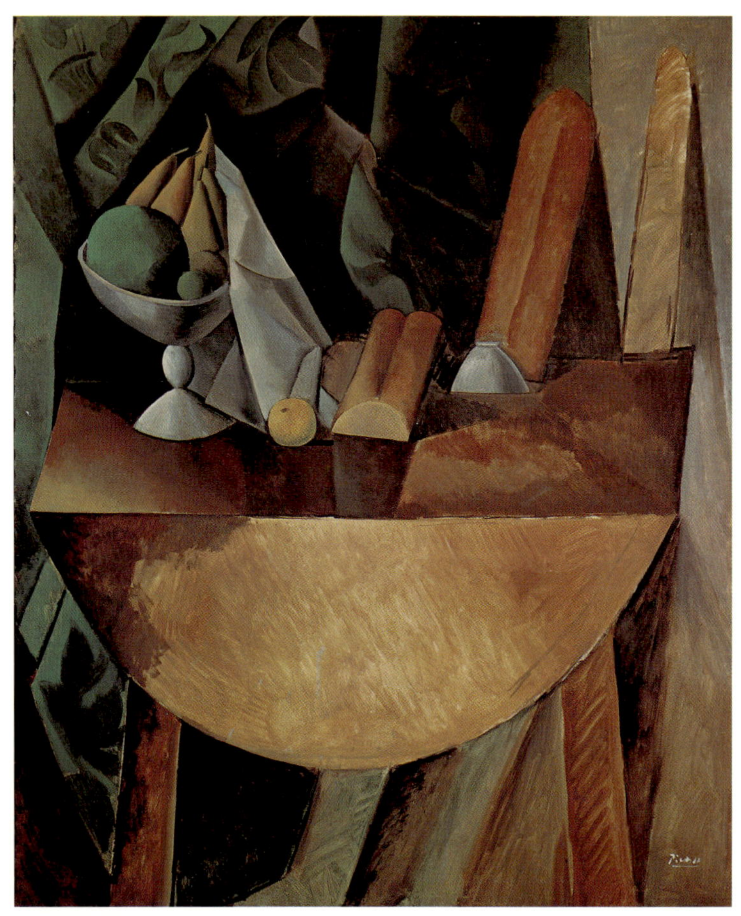

BREAD AND FRUIT DISH ON A TABLE, 1909. Picasso painted this still
life in the winter, in Paris, prior to his sojourn in Horta, but
it confronts some of the same issues as the canvases completed
later in the year. The complex representation of the table in
various planes and the curtain's geometric folds are precursors
to the Cubist pictorial schemes of the following years.

GIRL WITH A MANDOLIN, 1910. The subject matter of this painting is
fully within the Cubist repertory, but the new mode of expression
is still tentative. There is a tension between the lower part of the
canvas, which is still quite illusionistic in its depiction of the
mandolin, and the upper part, where there is more abstraction in
the juxtaposition of planes on the surface. The lack of definitive
borders is one of the problems that would be most difficult for
Cubism to resolve.

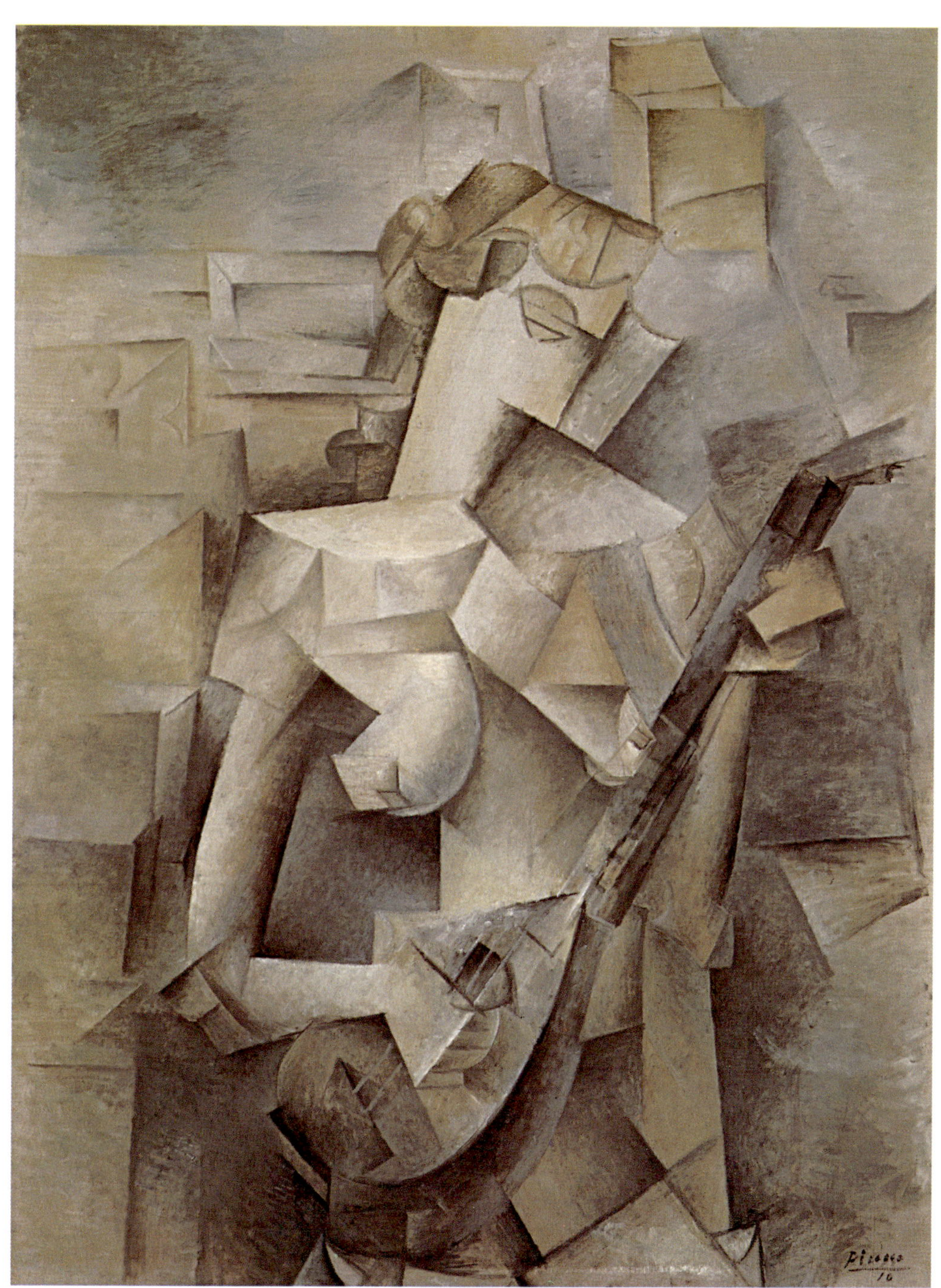

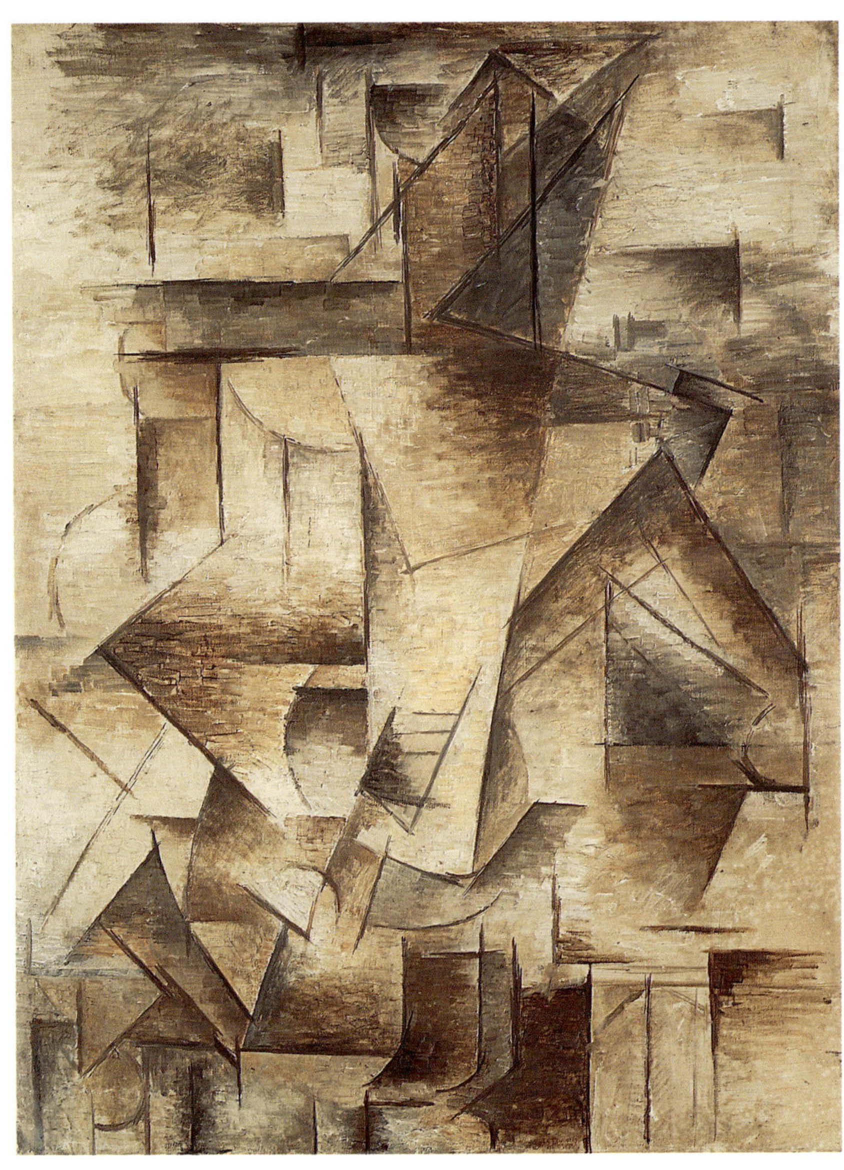

THE GUITARIST, 1910. The contrasts of color have disappeared completely and the canvas is reduced to a simple linear scheme delimited by the planes of the figure, soberly modulated with tiny brushstrokes. By opening up the composition, the artist attempts to lessen the bas-relief effect of the painting and integrate the borders within the surface of the canvas.

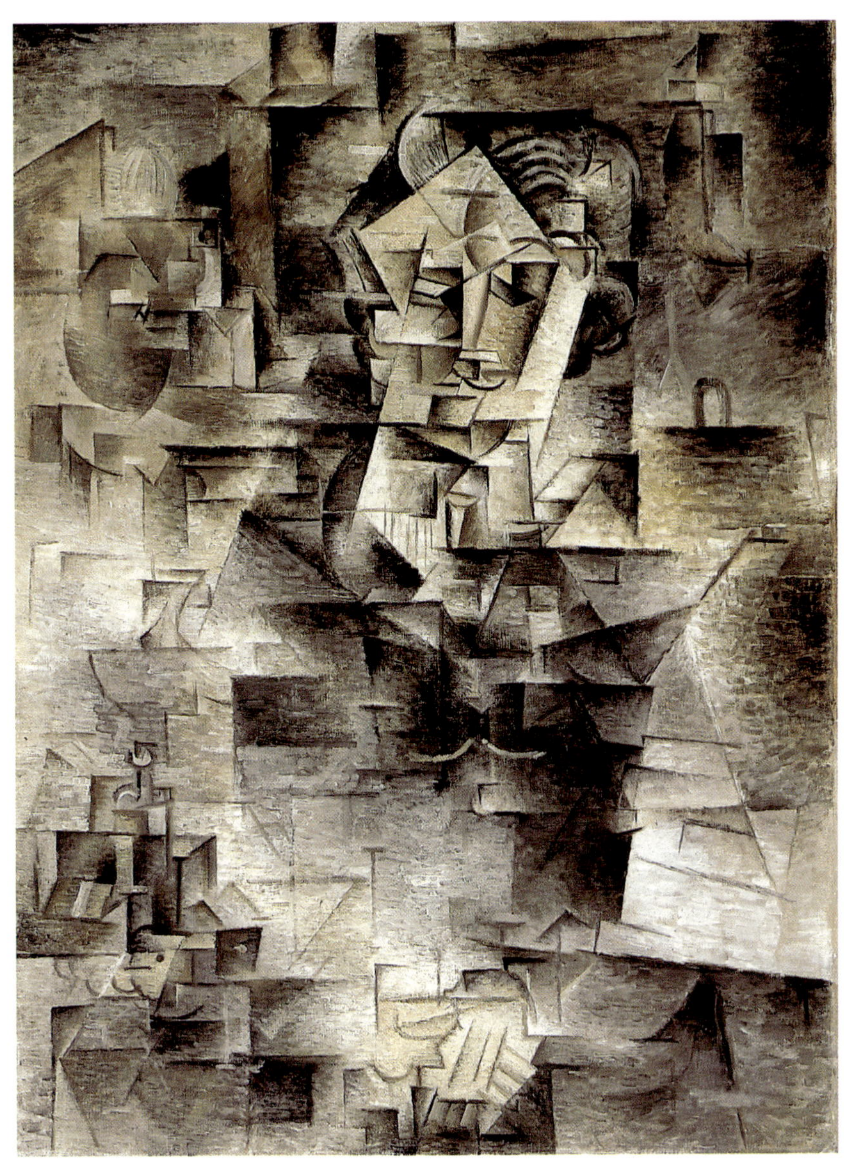

PORTRAIT OF DANIEL HENRY KAHNWEILER, 1910. D.H. Kahnweiler was a German dealer who backed Cubism from the very beginning. His portrait is one of the most successful paintings within the realm of Analytical Cubism. The nose, eyes, hands, and the bottle of the still-life to the right comprise the figurative clues that permit the viewer to reconstruct the image.

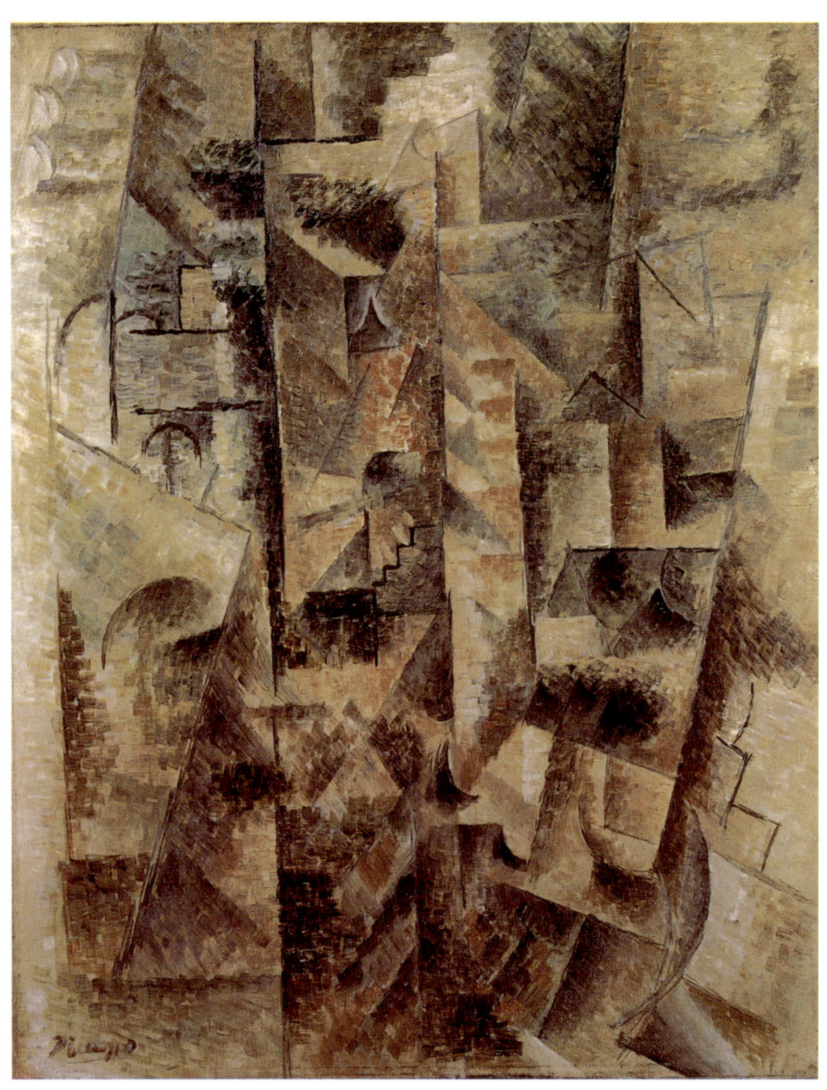

CÉRET LANDSCAPE, 1911. Picasso and Georges Braque spent the summer of 1911 painting together in the little town of Céret, located in the Pyrenees. Picasso's work from this period documents his experimentation with the homogeneous depiction of space on the canvas. This exploration lends the paintings of this period a flatter, more integrated appearance and makes their subject matter, which can hardly be recognized, much more difficult to interpret.

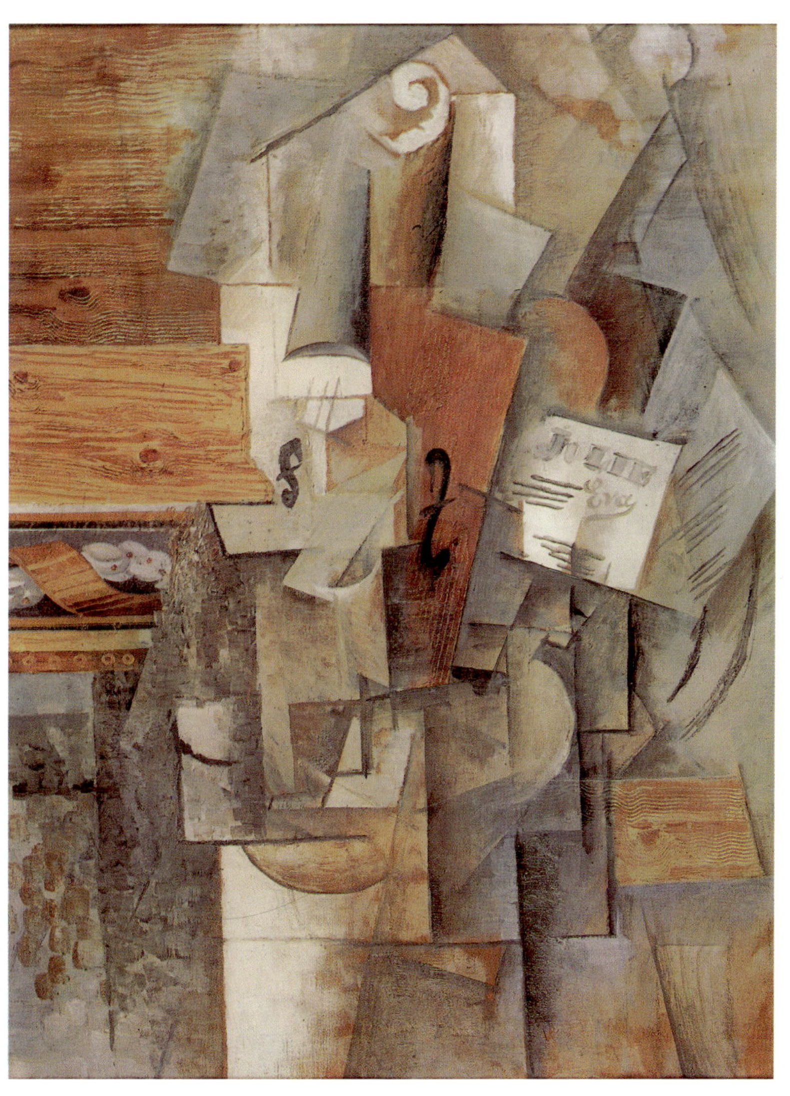

THE VIOLIN (JOLIE EVA), 1912.
The title refers to Marcelle
Humbert (Eva), Picasso's
companion during those years.
The imitation of the textures
of wood grain with paint is a
contribution by Georges Braque,
who had experience as a
decorator. This treatment
serves as a precedent for the
papiers collés, which first
appeared in 1912. The balance
of representation and the
planar configuration of space
epitomize the main achievement
of Analytical Cubism.

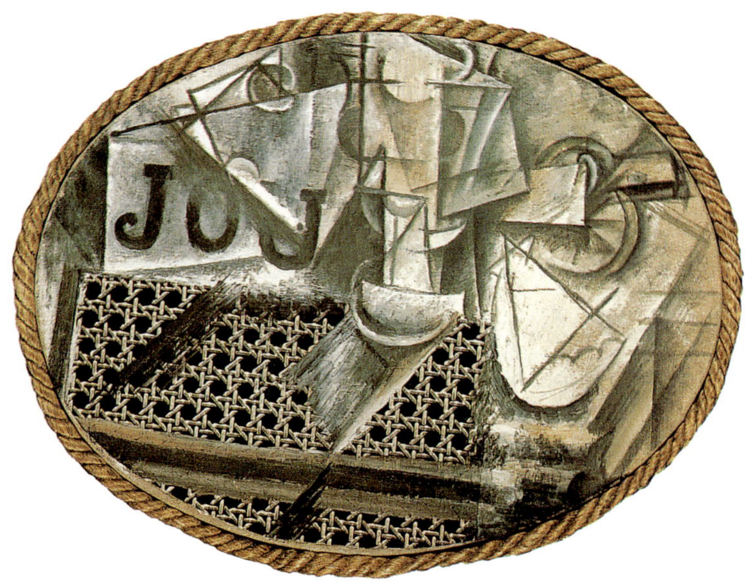

THE PAINTING AS OBJECT

By 1912 Cubist expression had matured to the point that it could
represent reality by means of non-naturalistic procedures. The next
step was taken by Picasso in that same year by incorporating a piece
of oilcloth in the guise of chair caning into a still-life. Thus were born
the *papiers collés*—glued-on papers—the first manifestation of the
collage. The application onto the canvas of any matter foreign to the
paint marks another of the great contributions of Cubism to modern
art. The relationship of the painting to reality becomes increasingly
complex, especially because Picasso applied these new artistic
gestures with great imagination and irony, avoiding the literal
correspondence between the object and its representation.
A piece of newspaper, for example, could be transformed into
a bottle or a chair, and also serve as the source for a visual pun.
Thus the painting itself becomes an object, one more element
of reality, endowed with specificity and autonomy.

STILL LIFE WITH CHAIR CANING,
1912. This canvas initiated
the technique of *papier collé*,
and with it a new twist in the
representation of reality within
painting. The oval format helps
to eliminate spatial ambiguity
around the edges.

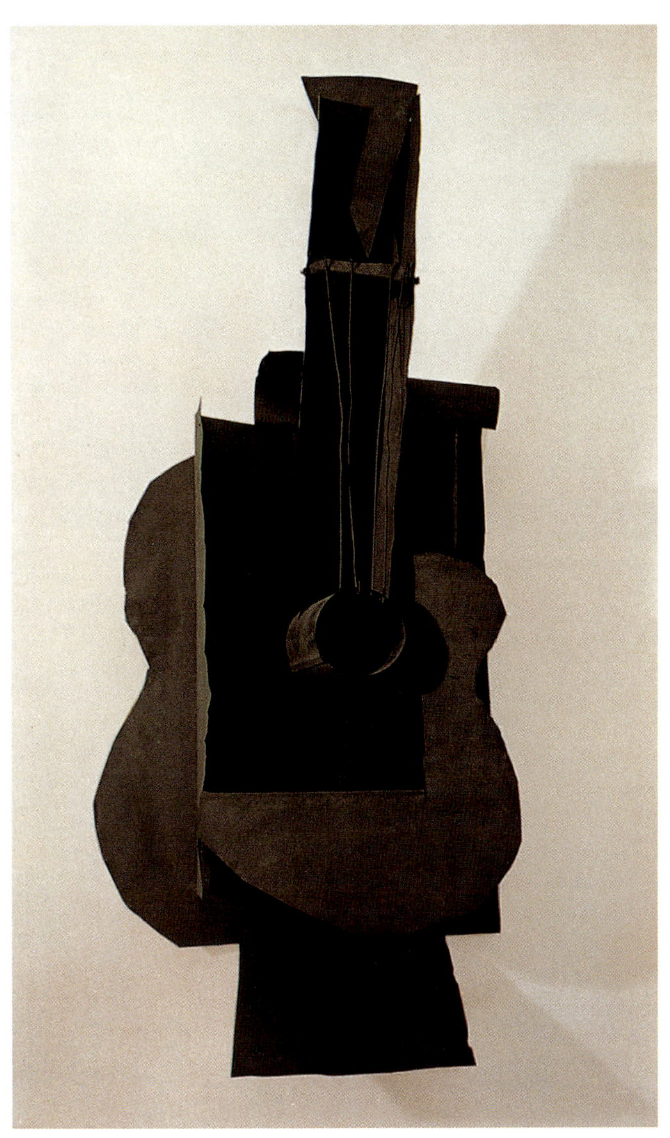

GUITAR, 1912. This collage
introduces ambiguous devices
that, apart from their own
importance, suggest new
possibilities for painting.
Hence, the inversion of solid
and void, and convex and
concave: part of the object
—the guitar body—is portrayed
by its absence, yet the central
opening, a void in reality, is
transformed into a projecting
cylinder.

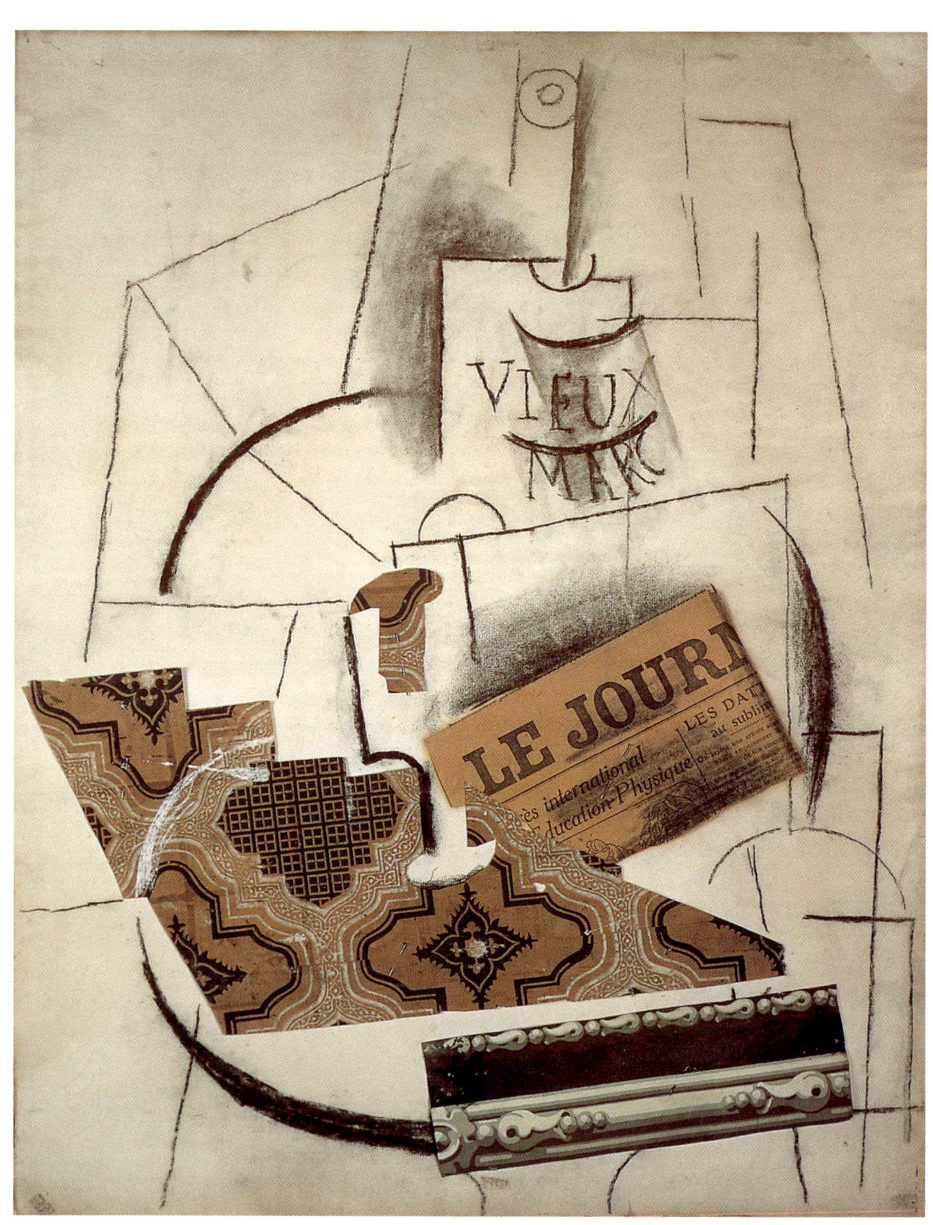

VIEUX
MARC
LE JOURN
LES DAT
ès international
au subli
Éducation Physique

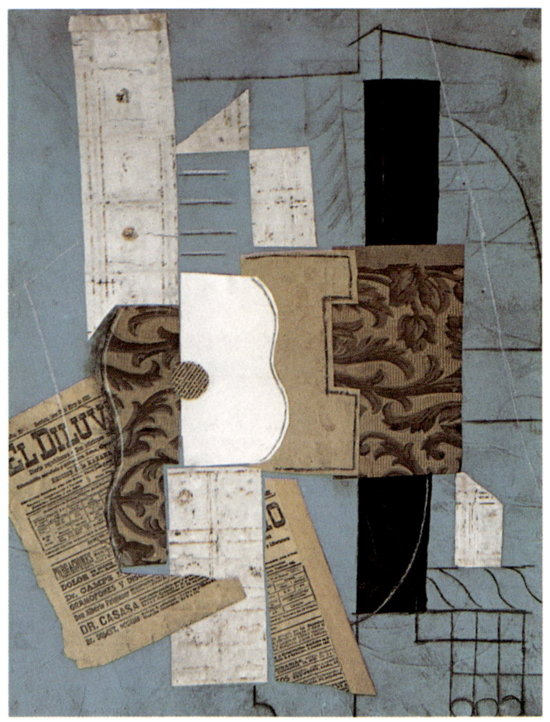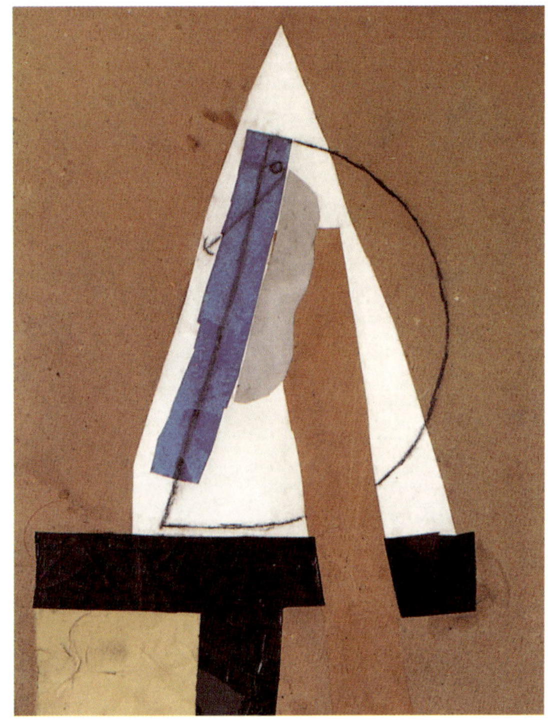

BOTTLE OF VIEUX MARC, GLASS, AND NEWSPAPER, 1913. Picasso extracts the maximum potential from *papiers collés:* while the newspaper represents a real newspaper beside the schematically drawn bottle, two pieces of wallpaper appear to be totally decontextualized and take on significations quite different from their typical association.

GUITAR, 1913. "If a piece of newspaper can become a bottle, that gives us something to think about with respect to both newspapers and bottles", affirmed Picasso about the objective nature of *papiers collés*. That displacement of objects is quite evident in the wallpaper forming the guitar in this composition.

HEAD, 1913. The experience with collage and *papier collé* helped Picasso cross the bridge from Analytic Cubism to Synthetic Cubism. In this case, the combination of a triangle and a semicircle produces a figurative association and not the reverse, in which figurative forms are reduced to abstraction, as had occurred before.

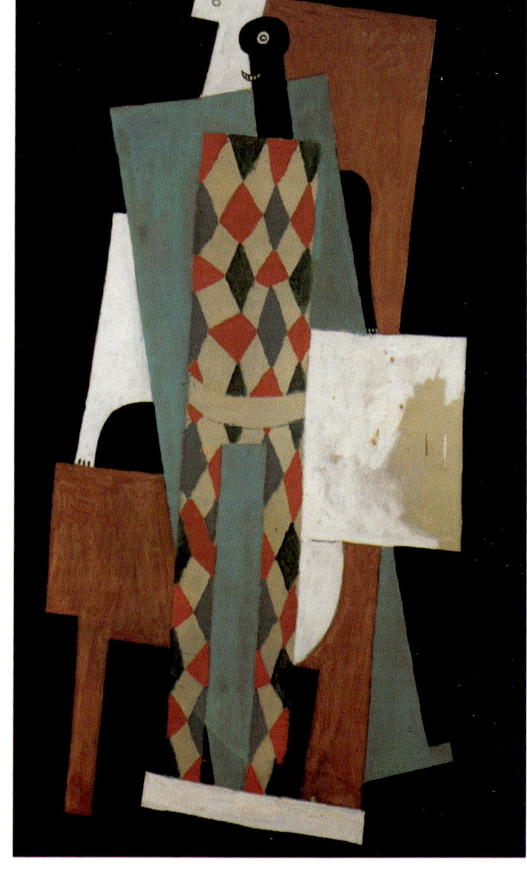

Following Georges Braque's enlistment in the armed forces
with the onset of World War I in 1914, Picasso continued
his quest alone. The conceptual autonomy of the painting
achieved with the *papiers collés* came to be a liberation, as
the dependence on the subject to drive the work was ever
more lessened. In fact, at this stage in Picasso's work, the
pictorial process inverts its terms. If the work could allow
different materials and textures, for the same reasons it
could allow the contrast of color. Thus, between 1914 and
1921 Picasso's canvases exhibit an extremely rich palette.
Using a combination of formal, chromatic structures and
different textures, figurative associations are attained. The
critics baptized this approach Synthetic Cubism, in opposition
to the analytical procedure of the previous paintings, which
constructed a pictorial order from data based on knowledge
of the painted object. Cubism thus came full circle and
established an artistic language of lasting universal value.

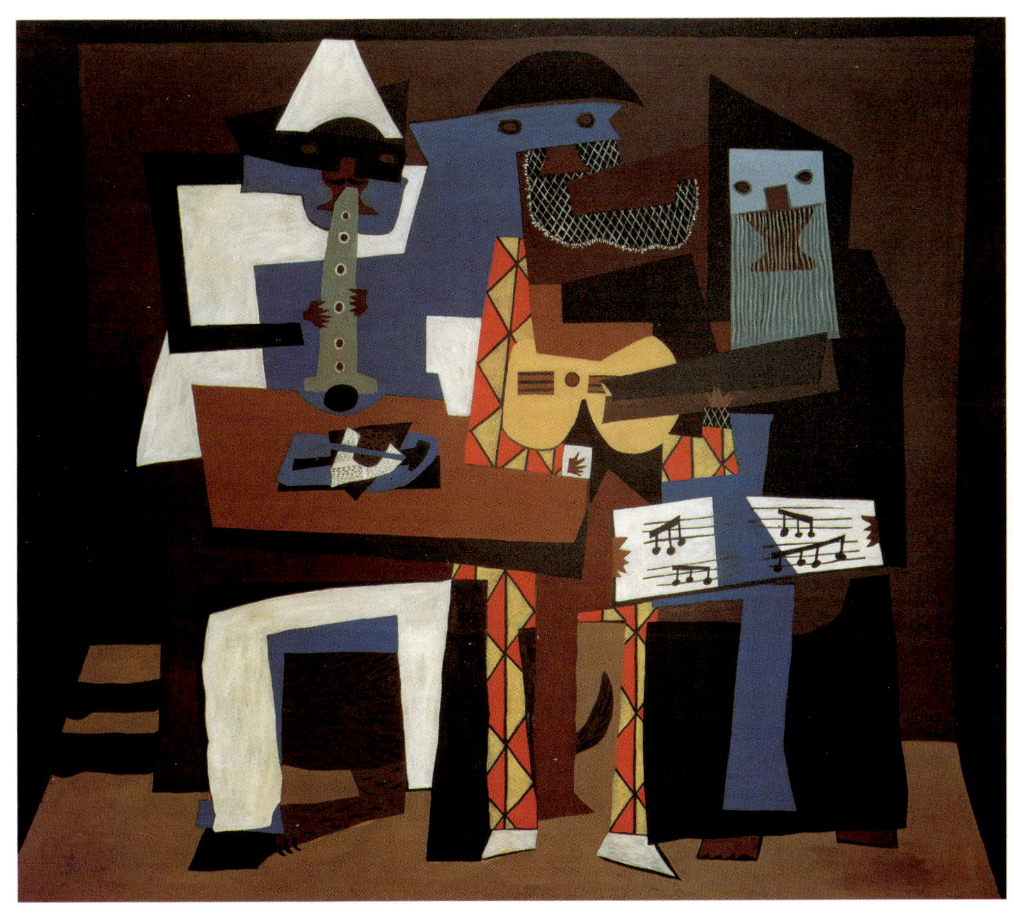

HARLEQUIN, 1915. A characteristic
example of the inversion of
the pictorial process
introduced by Synthetic Cubism:
displaced colored surfaces
are superimposed and slightly
skewed, suggesting the figure
of the harlequin, which is so
frequent in Picasso's canvases.

THREE MUSICIANS, 1921.
In contrast to the works
of Analytical Cubism, the
constructive rigor of these
paintings no longer excludes
the incorporation of color or
a certain decorative sense that
Picasso learned from his work
for Diaghilev's Ballets Russes.
The painter's fidelity to themes
like the *commedia dell'arte* was
strong in this period.

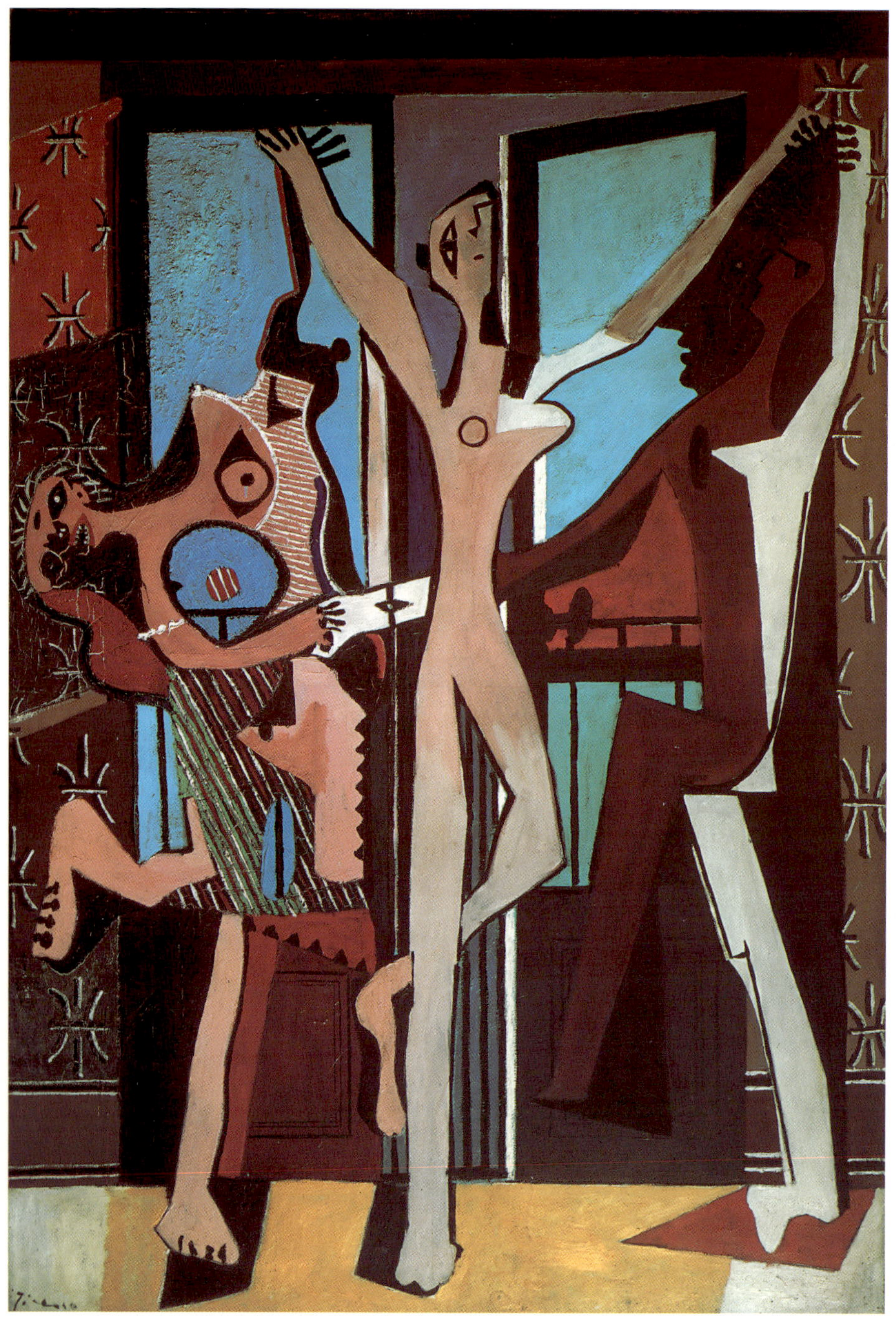

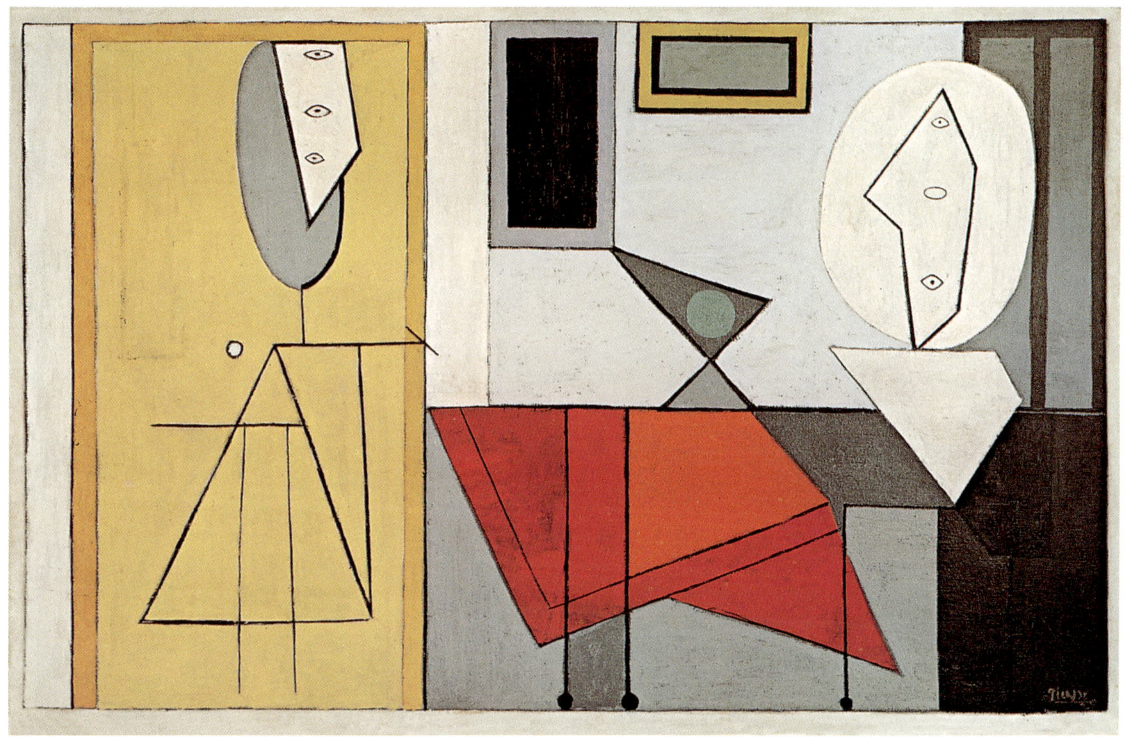

THE DANCE, 1925. Apparently
this painting is partly a
tribute to Ramon Pitxot, who
had died shortly before. Some
of the expressionist tone of
the 1930s is foreshadowed here,
although the most dominant
quality of the work is the
rhythmic and *syncopated*
composition, not unlike the
style of Art Deco decorative
panels, whose origins are
to be found in canvases like
this one.

THE STUDIO, 1927-28. The last
works that can be characterized
as Cubist stand out because
of their exacting precision
and flat abstraction, always
achieved with a minimum of
elements. Thus, Picasso brought
to a conclusion the arduous,
experimental task undertaken
twenty years earlier in
Les Demoiselles d'Avignon.

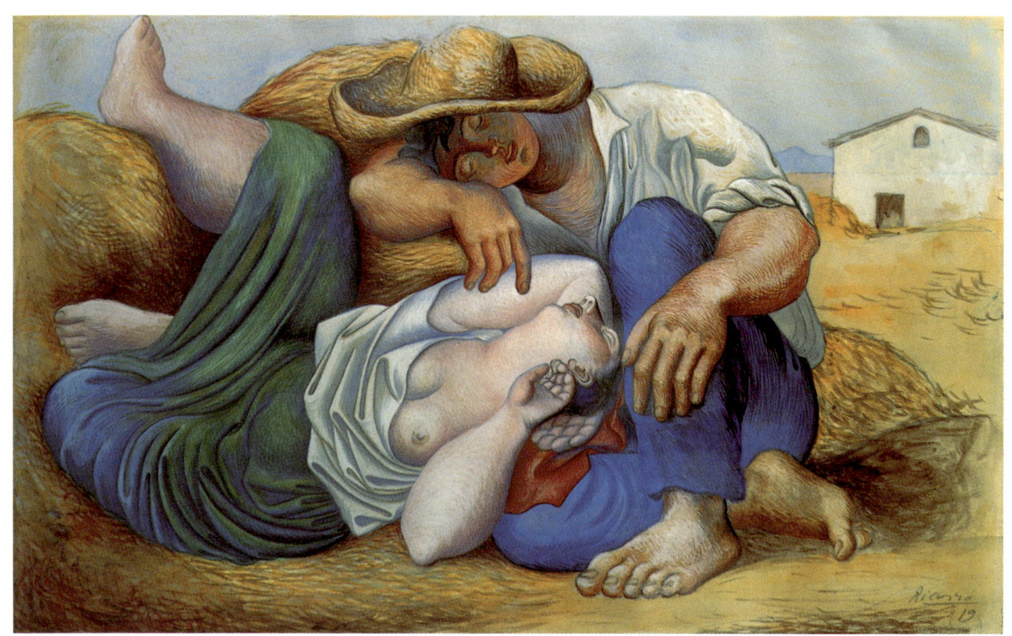

THE RETURN TO ORDER

Following World War I, the artistic scene in Paris seemed to take a rest after the intense outpouring of innovation in the first two decades of the century. For a few years the artistic culture experienced a certain return to traditional values, a trend to which Picasso was not alien. At that time the Spanish painter considered Cubism a complementary alternative that enlarged the domain of painting, but which did not invalidate traditional figurative art. Thus, between 1917 and 1923, Picasso, alternating with Cubist canvases, practiced a certain Mediterranean classicism that revived his interest in form in almost sculptural terms. The influence of Jean-Auguste-Dominique Ingres, the great nineteenth-century French Romantic Classicist, is evident in the precision and discipline of Picasso's drawing from this period. At the end of the 1920s and the beginning of the 1930s Picasso introduced fantastic elements into otherwise conventional pictorial spaces. This, together with the refutation of established reality implicit in the collages, stimulated the interest of the Surrealists in Picasso's work.

SLEEPING PEASANTS, 1919. Despite the rotund solidity of the figures, the painting's composition is a delicate arabesque of concentric forms that close on themselves in a spiral, creating a specifically pictorial space that is not incompatible with naturalistic representation.

WOMAN IN SPANISH COSTUME, 1917. The frontal pose of the model and the fluid precision of the drawing have their origin in the portraits of women by J.-A.-D. Ingress. The pointillist color scheme is a means Picasso had already employed in the Cubist paintings of 1913 and 1914, when his palette began to become diversified.

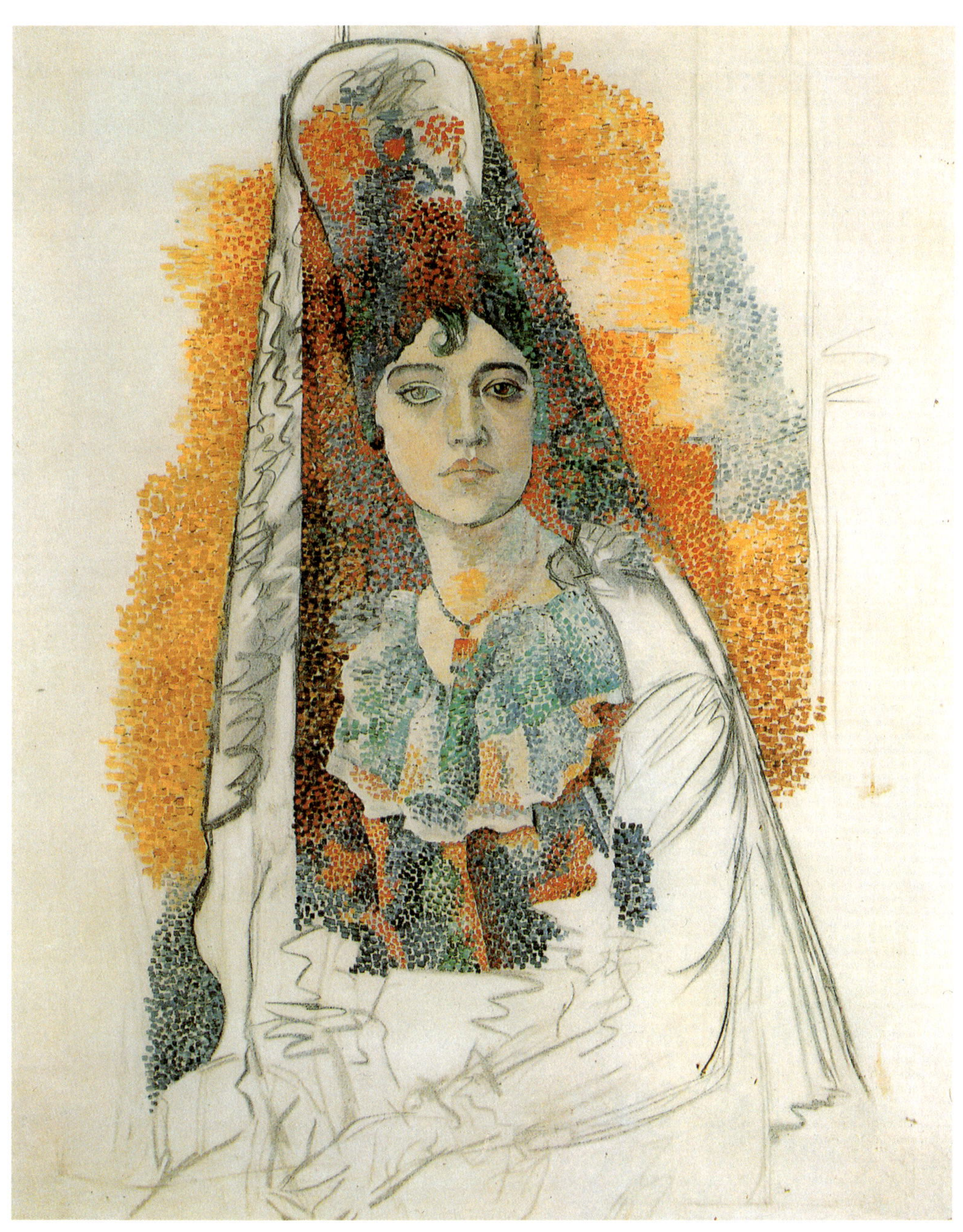

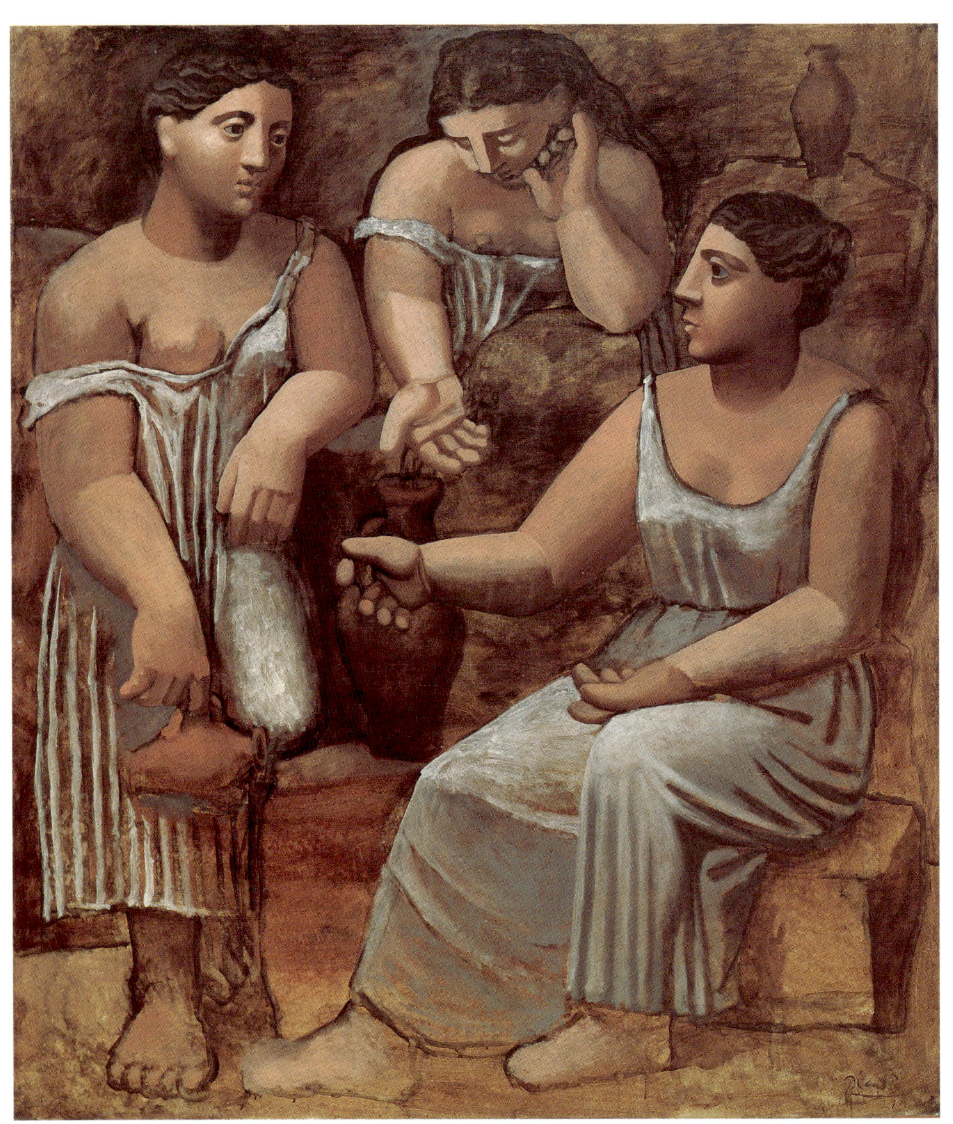

THREE WOMEN AT THE SPRING, 1921. The figurative format recalls
the work of the Blue Period, yet the monumentality reinforces the
sculptural quality of Picasso's figurative canvases during these
years. A classical reference is very evident in the pyramidal
composition of the group and in the figures' subtle gestures.
The classically-inspired, pleated tunics evoke the fluted Doric
columns of a Greek temple.

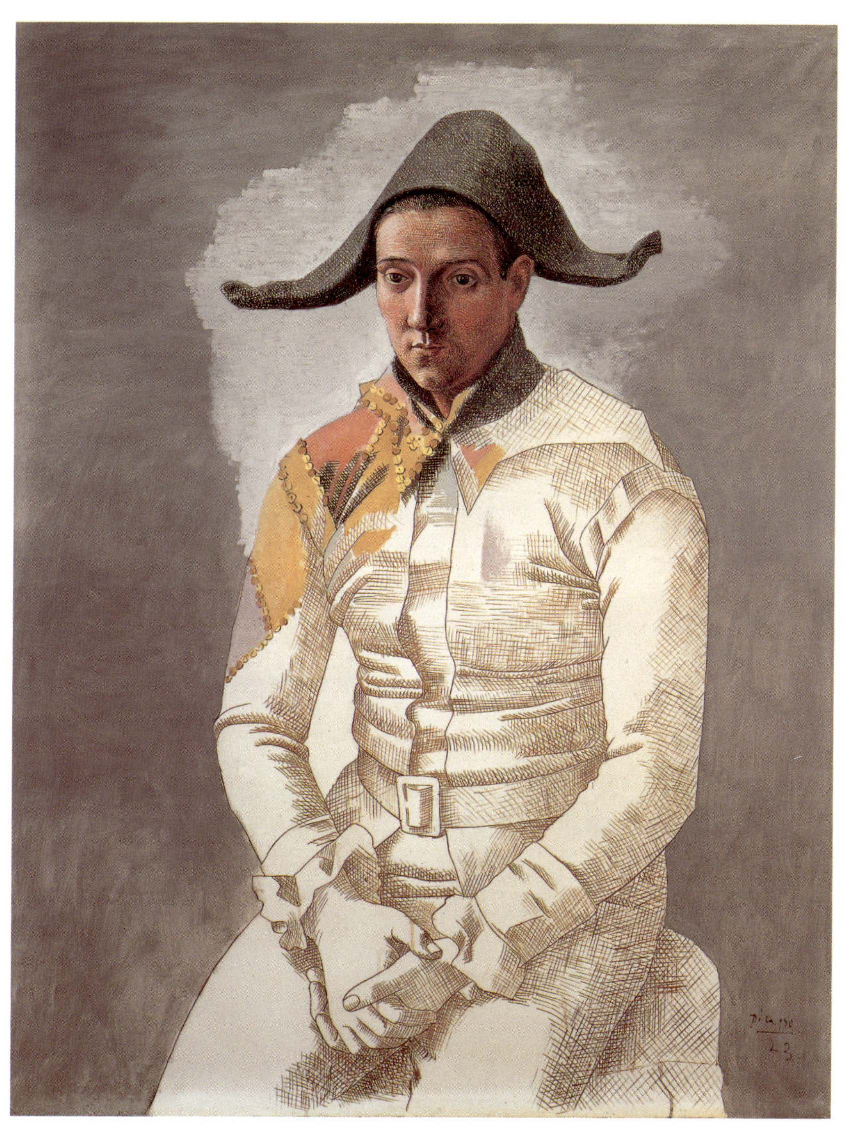

HARLEQUIN, 1923. The model for this portrait was the Catalan painter Jacint Salvadó, a friend of Picasso. The main character of the Italian *commedia dell'arte* always attracted the painter because of its expressive quality. The contrast between the modeled, colored area and the flatter sketch shows Picasso's experimentation in the representation of three-dimensional form, a dominant concern in the figurative work of this period.

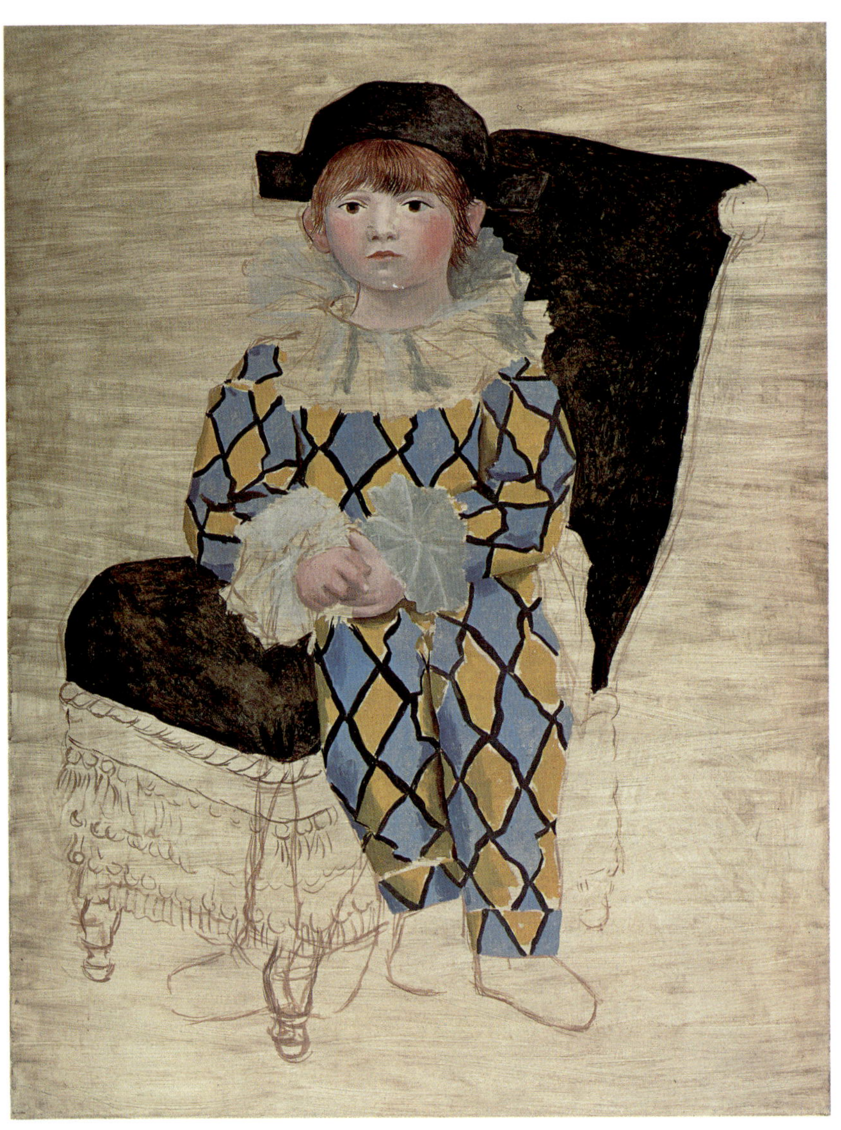

PAULO AS HARLEQUIN, 1924. Paulo, Picasso's oldest son from his marriage to ballerina Olga Koklova, was three years old at the time of this portrait. Picasso returned to the theme of the harlequin, which on this occasion is treated in a manner recalling the precise drawing of J.-A.-D. Ingres. The proportions and the composition of the figure in the space recall, nonetheless, *The Fife* by Edouard Manet and Philip IVs buffoons by Velázquez.

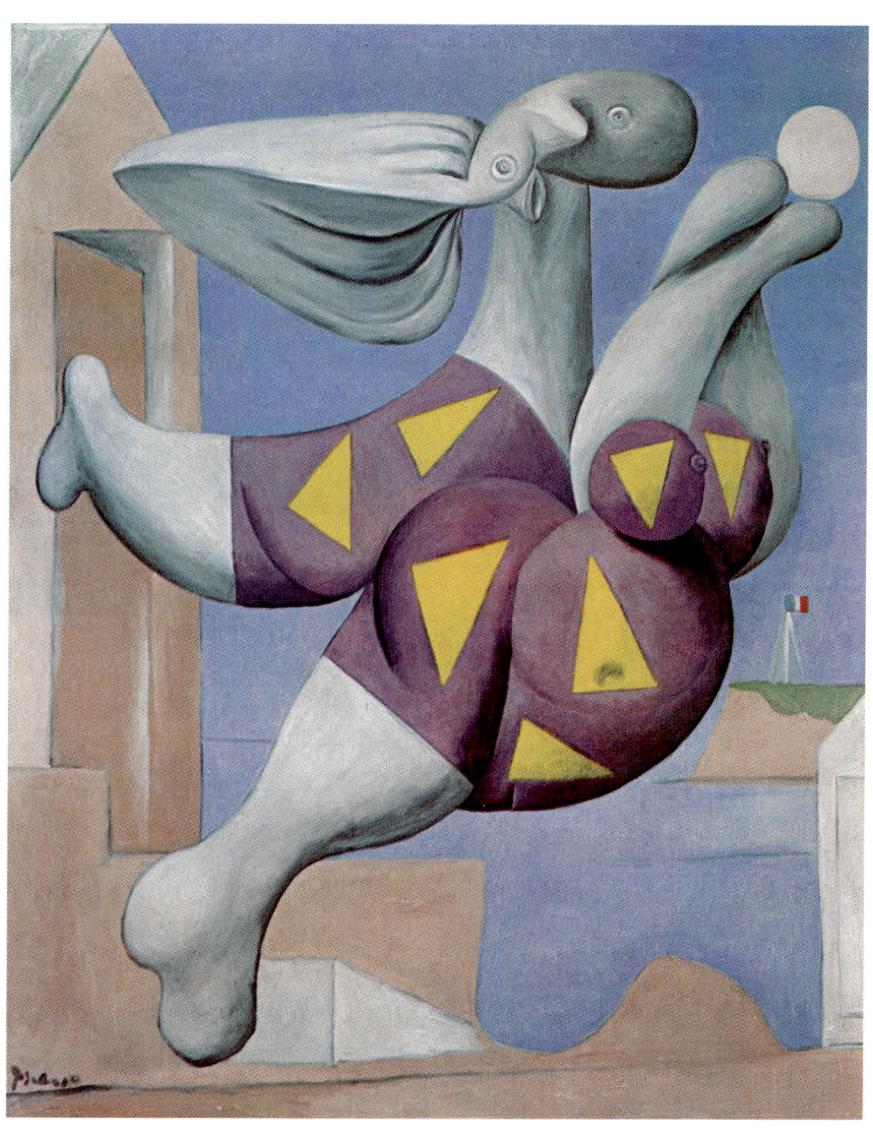

BATHER WITH BEACH BALL, 1932. In the late 1920s and early 1930s
Picasso began to employ devices appropriated from Cubism—such as
the overlapping of points of view—in traditional pictorial spaces.
This type of painting stimulated the interest of the Surrealists,
for whom Picasso had provided conceptual inspiration with collages
and *papiers collés*.

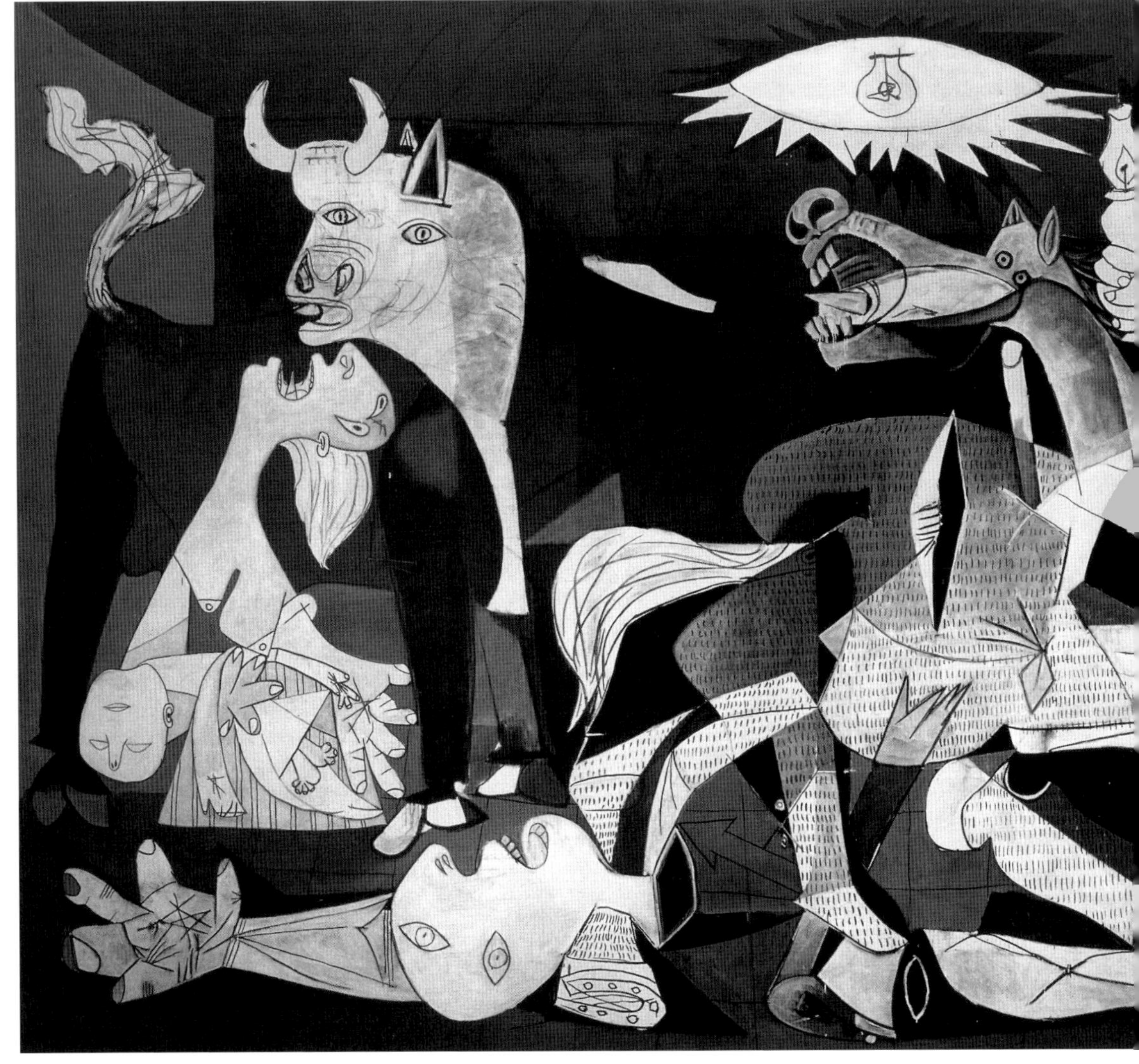

EXPRESSIONISM AND THE WAR

For Spanish artists residing in Paris, such as Joan Miró and Picasso, the decades of the 1930s and 1940s were years of continual upheaval because of the Spanish Civil War and World War II. Picasso's commitment to Spain's legitimate Republican regime heightened the painter's sensitivity to his national heritage. Cubism's devices, like the overlapping of the face both directly and in profile, were now used by Picasso with expressionistic techniques in order to evoke the horror of war. The peculiar Picassoesque expressionism which developed in this period is encountered later in the work of other, more recent painters like Francis Bacon or Lucien Freud. This period's touchstone is the monumental canvas, *Guernica* (1937), painted in reaction to the devastating bombardment perpetrated by the German military on a small Basque town. This great mural was the star attraction of the Spanish Pavilion in the 1937 World's Fair in Paris, to which artists like Joan Miró, Alberto Sánchez, Julio González, Alexander Calder, and Josep Lluís Sert (the architect in charge of the project, along with Luis Lacasa) also contributed.

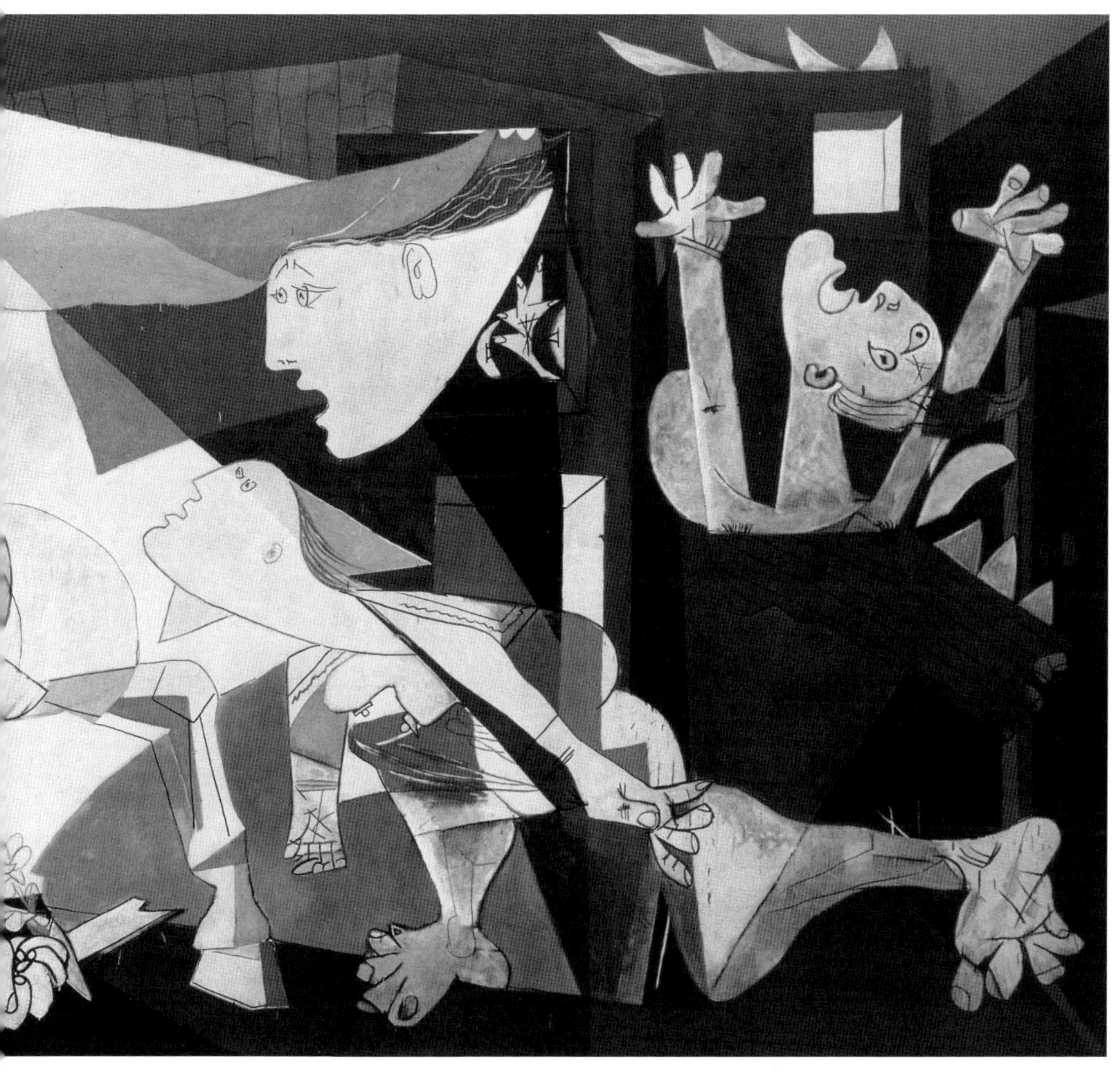

GUERNICA, 1937. The German air force bombed Guernica on April 26, 1937, prompting a massacre of the civilian population. Picasso was so moved by this tragedy that in just less than a month he had completed this monumental work, preceded by a great number of sketches and preparatory studies. A series of emblematic figures evokes the horror of the event: the bull, the wounded horse—symbolizing the innocent civilian victims—the decapitated warrior, the wail of a mother with her dead child in her arms. The composition of the space is Cubist in origin, as is the treatment of many of the figures. The renunciation of color also has an expressive function. Never since *The Death of Marat* by Jacques-Louis David or *The Massacre at Chios* by Eugène Delacroix, had painting achieved such a universal expression of the drama of contemporary events.

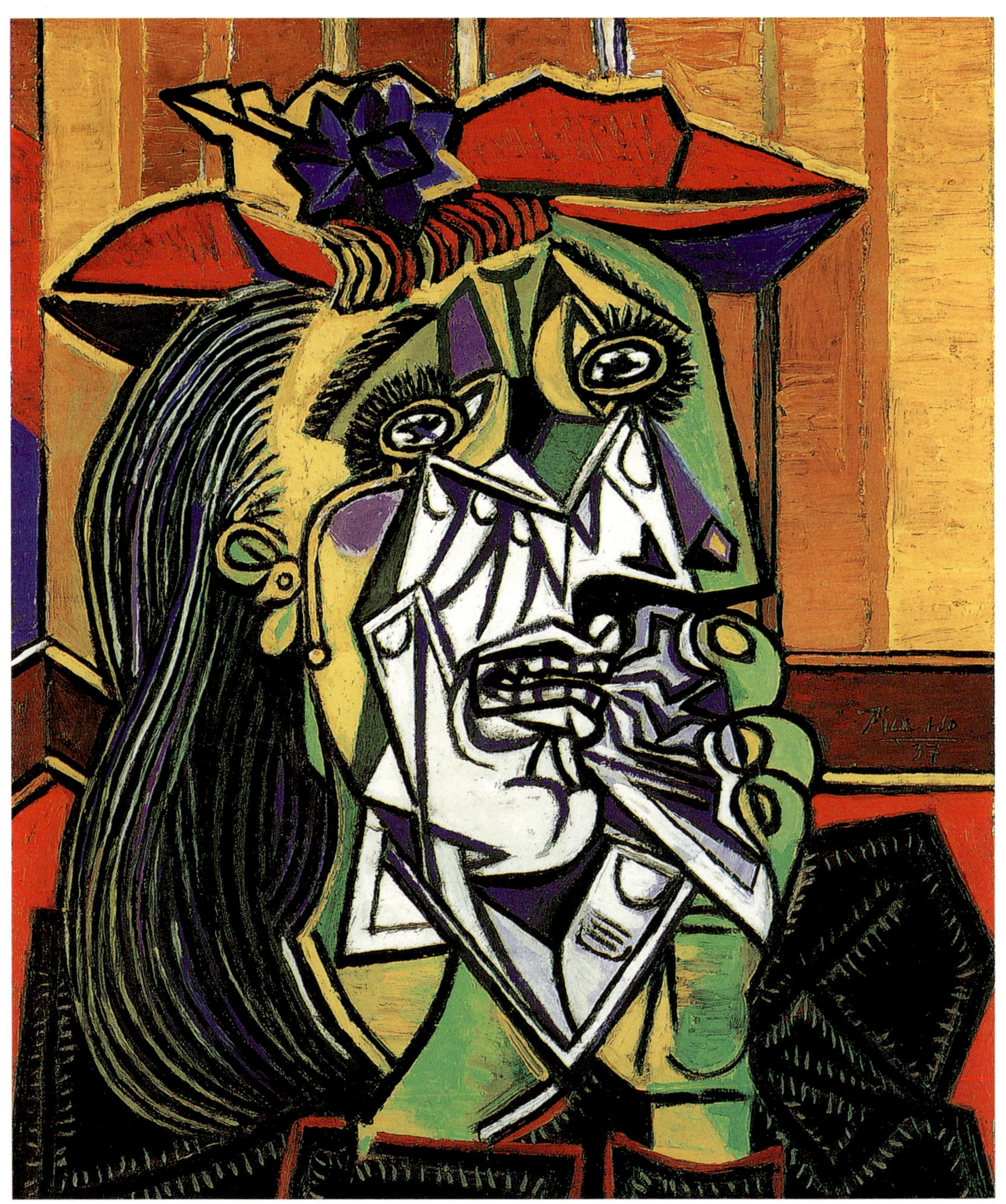

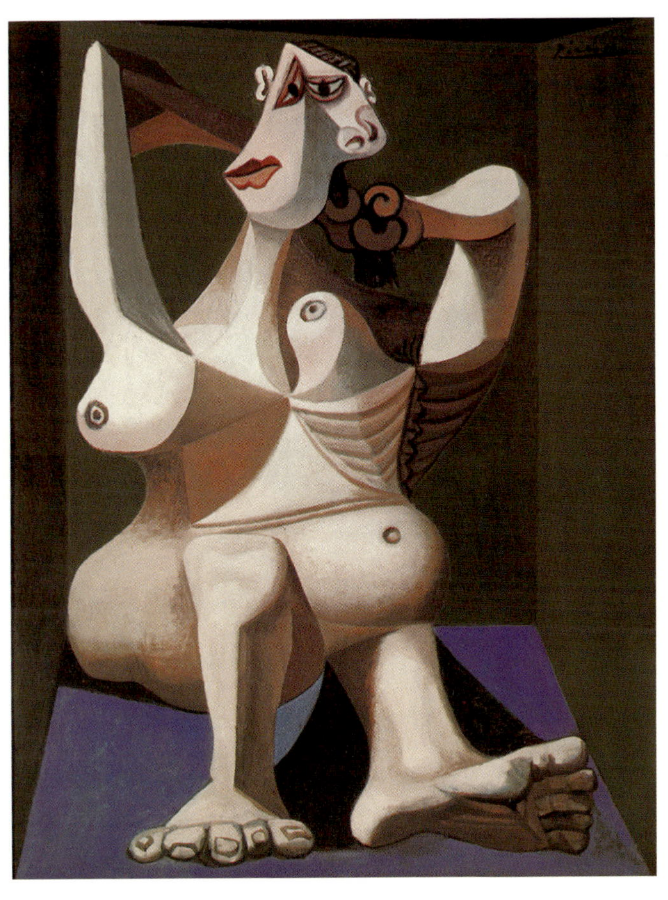

WEEPING WOMAN, 1937.
The expressive devices employed
in *Guernica* again return to
the canvas. Color—greens and
acrid yellows— also have
an expressionist function in
Picasso's work of those years,
much of which was dedicated to
conveying the heightened drama
and tension of the era.

WOMAN DRESSING HER HAIR, 1940. The composition recalls the
surrealistic scenes of the late 1920s and the early 1930s:
a traditional orthogonal space inhabited by an unsetling figure
taken from Cubism, which is no longer an experimental method,
but rather an expressive means to evoke monsters.

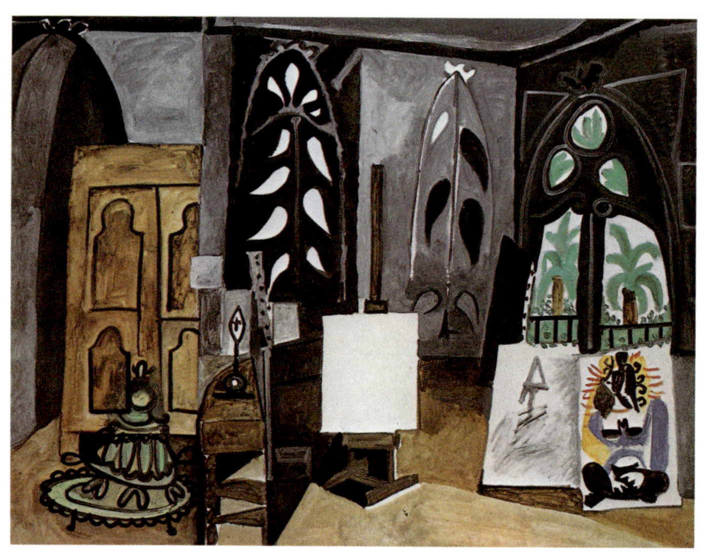

THE MAIDS OF HONOR (LAS MENINAS)

From among Picasso's abundant output in the postwar period, two interrelated series of paintings are particularly significant. The 1956 work *The Studio* (series) and *The Maids of Honor (Las Meninas)* of the following year represent interior views of his house and studio of La Californie, in Cannes, where he had lived with Françoise Gilot, the mother of his two youngest children. During the years in which these works were painted, the period between breaking up with Françoise and establishing a relationship with his last companion, Jacqueline Roque, Picasso found himself alone. Solitude—to which the painter was not accustomed—led him to re-create those quiet, intimate interiors, empty yet bathed in dazzling Mediterranean light. On a few occasions such as this one, Picasso surrendered to the pure pleasure of painting, lingering on the vibration of color on the canvas, almost as in the paintings of Henri Matisse to whom *The Studio* series pays homage. Velázquez served Picasso as an intermediary in *The Maids of Honor (Las Meninas)*, an homage that the painter used to veil the autobiographical quality of the paintings.

THE STUDIO OF LA CALIFORNIE. 1956. Space is re-created in strictly visual terms, using solid patches of color extended over the canvas, which is left white and without prior priming.

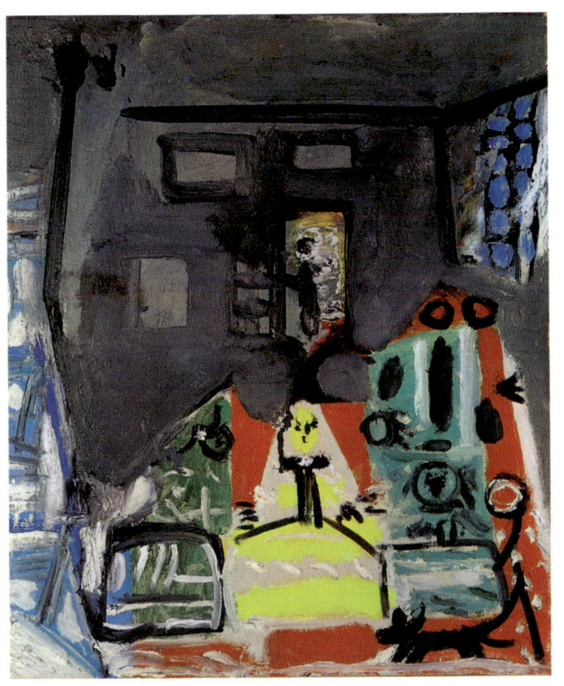

THE MAIDS OF HONOR (LAS
MENINAS), AFTER VELÁZQUEZ, 1957.
Color individualizes the figures
against the gray and bluish
tones of the room's shadows.

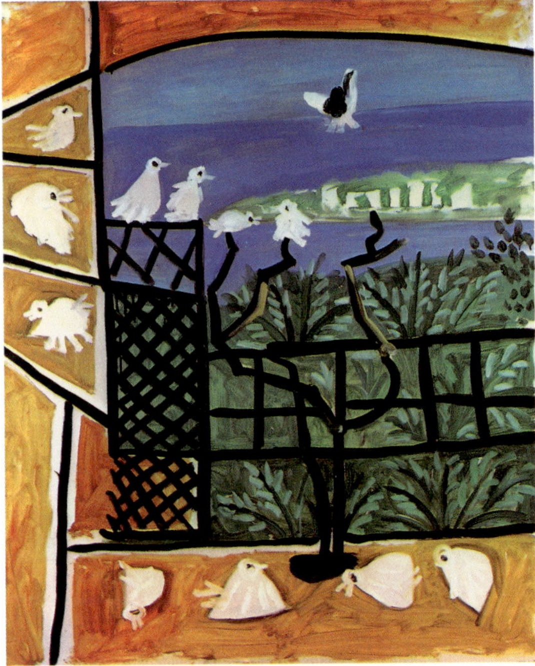

LAS MENINAS (THE DOVES, 1),
1957. Picasso's fixation with
doves goes back to his
childhood in Málaga, where
his father often used them
as a subject in his drawings.

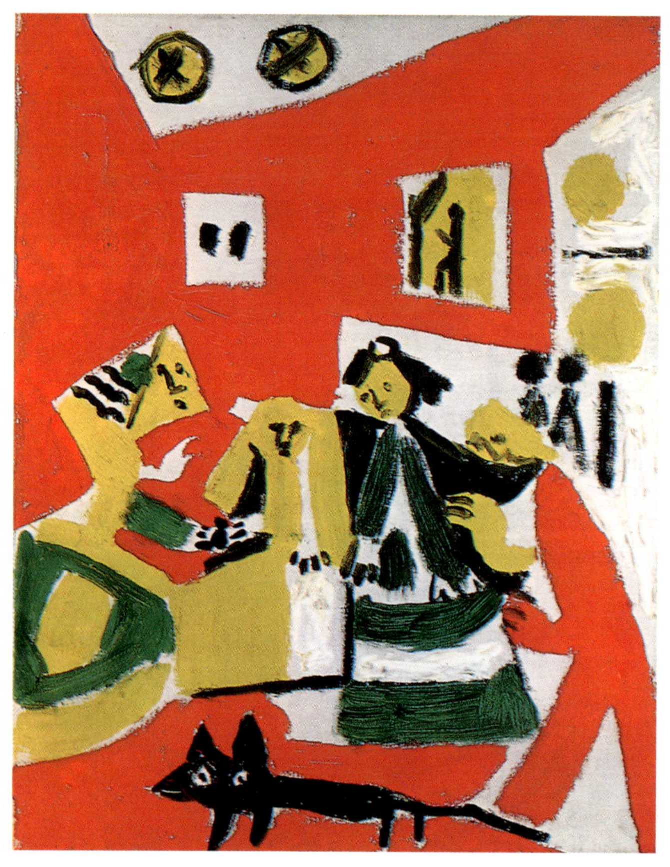

THE MAIDS OF HONOR (LAS MENINAS), 1957. The saturated red background against which the figures float recalls certain paintings by Henri Matisse, with whom Picasso had frequent contact during the years spent in Nice.

LAS MENINAS, 1957. The last painting of the series most closely follows the dark, luminous hues and fluid brushstrokes of Velázquez.

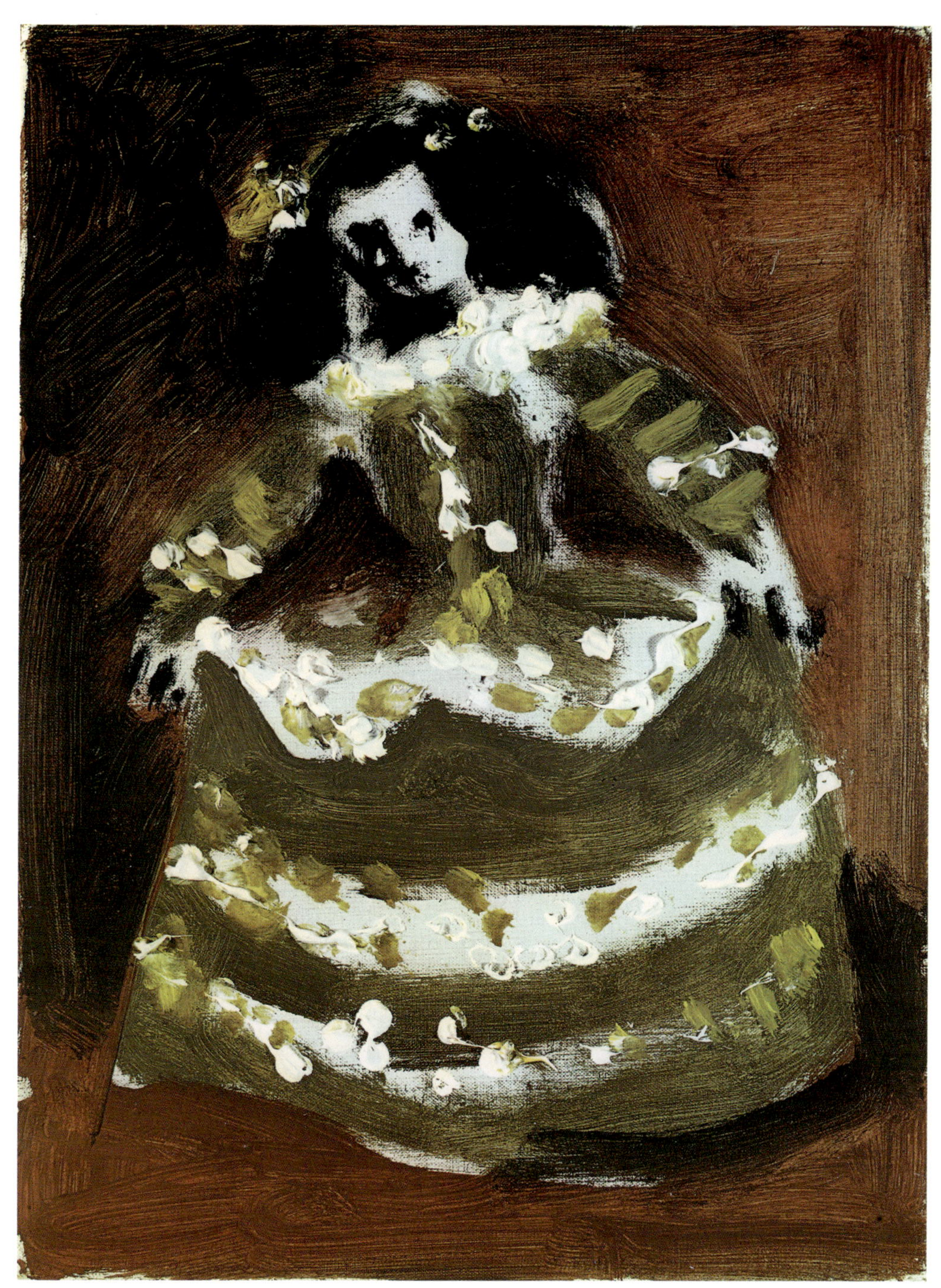

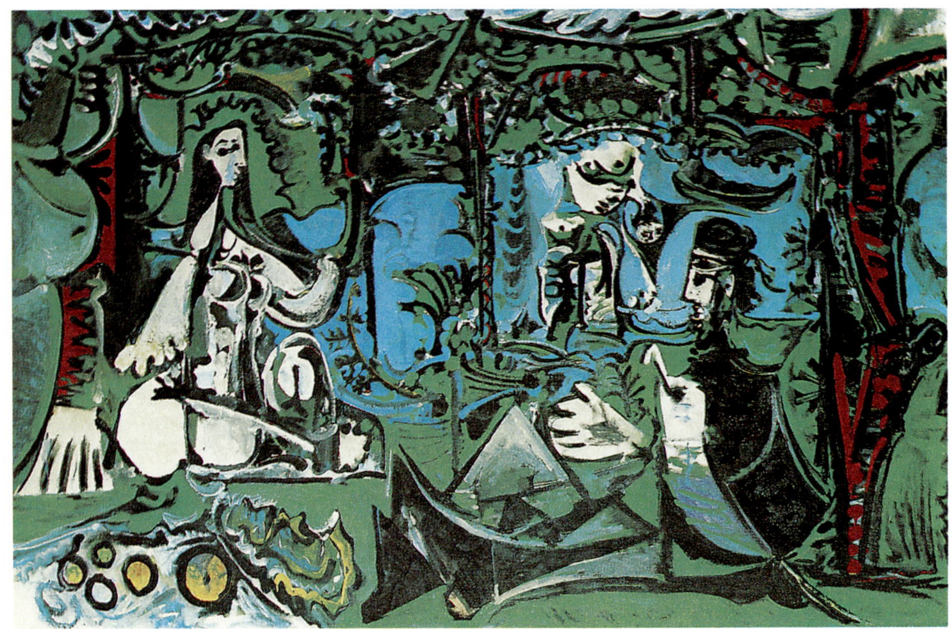

THE FREEDOM OF PAINTING

The last years of Picasso's life and work bequeathed to posterity an image of mythic vitality, difficult to imagine in a man who died at the age of ninety-two. His creative production between 1960 and 1973 is quite extensive and encompasses all mediums, from linoleum engraving and etching to easel painting and sculpture. The common denominator in his late work is the freedom of execution. From the re-creation of past masters to a jovial use of color or caricaturesque expressionism, the mastery that accompanied Picasso from his youthful, academic studies was now transformed into an authentic celebration of painting in itself.

LUNCHEON ON THE GRASS, AFTER MANET, 1960. Picasso re-created the famous painting by Edouard Manet, using a similar chromatic scale, but darker and colder, and reproducing its horizontal composition with bands of color.

WOMAN WITH HAT, 1962. The linoleum cuts represent one of the few innovations in technique from Picasso's later period as was customary, the painter extracted the maximum impact from the graphic possibilities of this procedure. The visual force of the image is attained by the fusion of drawing and color into a single gesture.

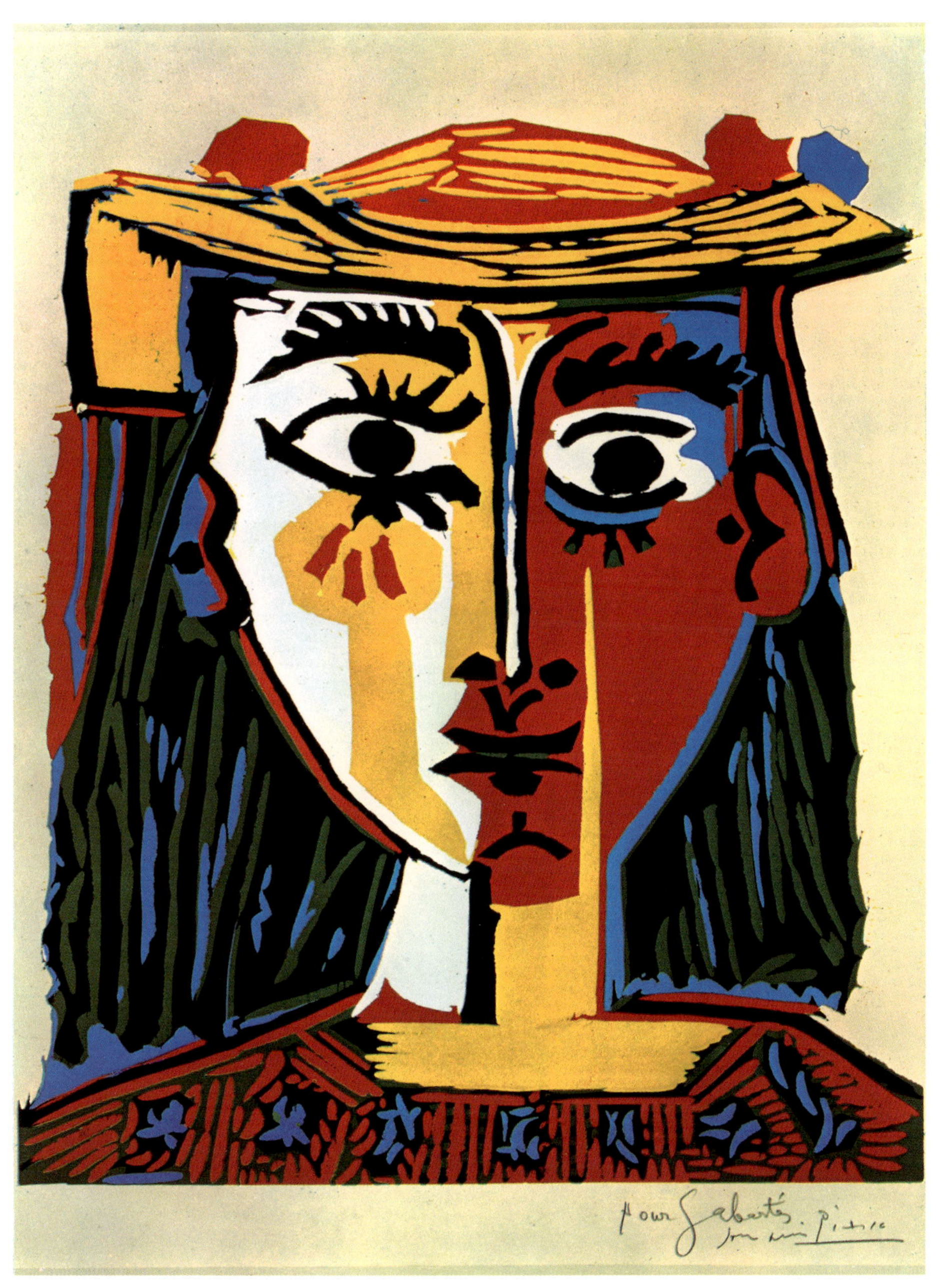

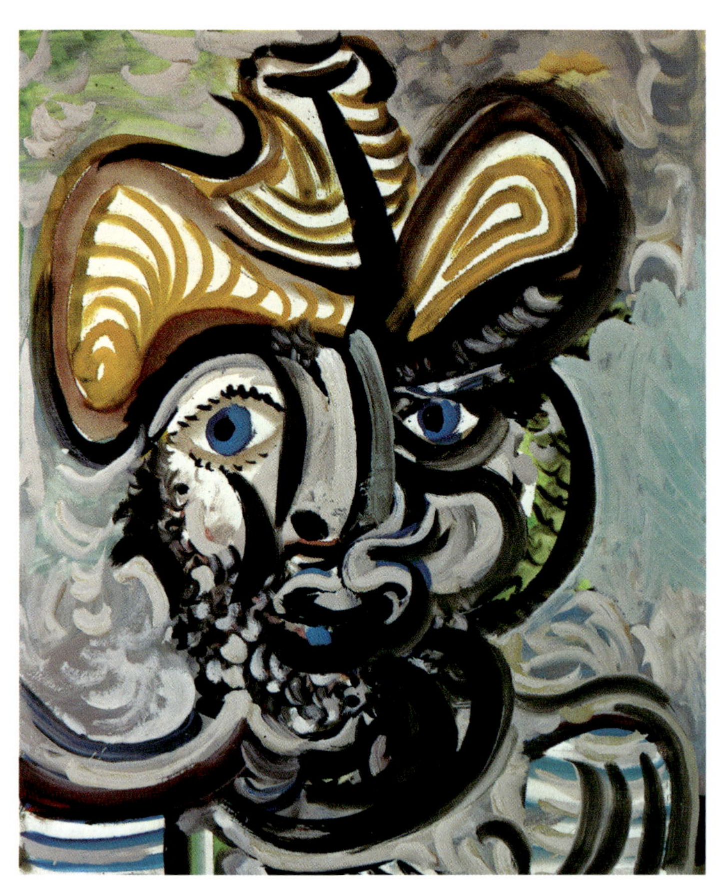

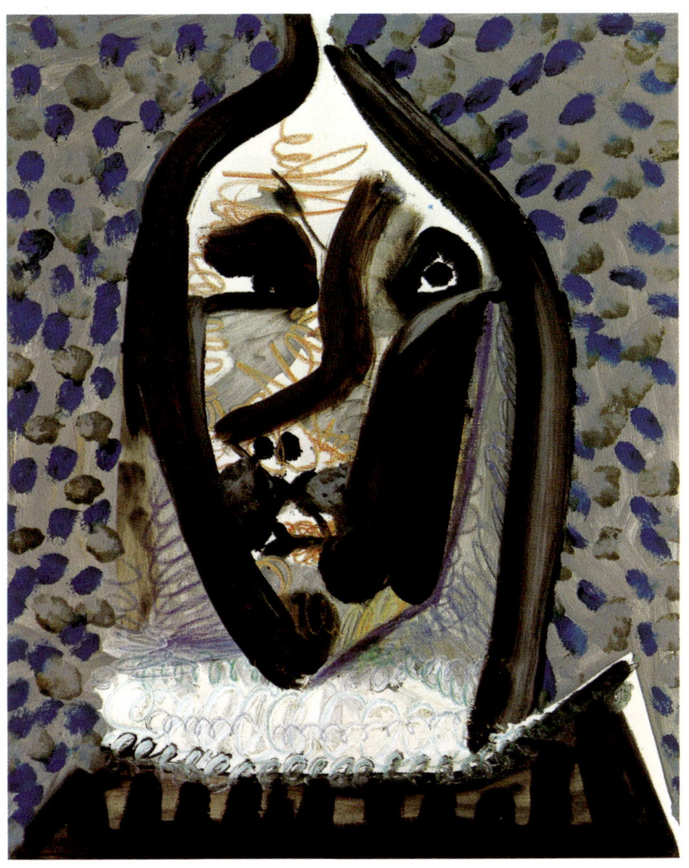

CHARACTER, 1972. HEAD OF A MAN, 1972. These two busts, painted
barely a year before Picasso's death, constitute pure recreation
in the mastery of pictorial gesture. Despite their apparent
spontaneity, the degree of control in drawing and composition
is extraordinary for a ninety-year-old.

p 50
Céret Landscape. Céret, Summer
1911.
Oil on canvas, 65 × 50 cm.
The Solomon R. Guggenheim
Museum, New York.

p 51
The Violin (Jolie Eva). Céret, Spring
1912.
Oil on canvas, 81 × 60 cm.
Staatsgalerie, Stuttgart.

p 52
Still Life with Chair Caning. Paris,
May 1912.
Collage of oil, oilcloth, and paper
on canvas (oval), framed with paper,
29 × 37 cm.
Musée Picasso, Paris.

p 53
Guitar. Paris, early 1912.
Sheet metal and wire,
77.5 × 35 × 19.3 cm.
The Museum of Modern Art,
New York. Gift of the artist.

p 54
**Bottle of Vieux Marc, Glass,
and Newspaper.** Céret, 1913.
Charcoal and pasted paper,
63 × 49 cm.
Musée National d'Art Moderne,
Centre Georges Pompidou, Paris.

p 55
Guitar. Céret, Spring 1913.
Charcoal, crayon, ink, and pasted
paper, 66.3 × 49.5 cm.
The Museum of Modern Art, New
York. Nelson A. Rockefeller Bequest.

p 55
Head. Paris or Céret, early 1913.
Charcoal and pasted paper on
cardboard, 43.5 × 33 cm.
Private Collection, London.

p 56
Harlequin. Paris, late 1915.
Oil on canvas, 183.5 × 105.1 cm.
The Museum of Modern Art,
New York. Acquired through the
Lillie P. Bliss Bequest.

p 57
Three Musicians. Fontainebleau,
Summer 1921.
Oil on canvas, 200.7 × 222.9 cm.
The Museum of Modern Art, New
York. Mrs. Simon Guggenheim Fund.

p 58
The Dance. Monte Carlo, June 1925.
Oil on canvas, 215 × 142 cm.
The Tate Gallery, London.

p 59
The Studio. Paris, Winter 1927-28.
Oil on canvas, 149.9 × 231.2 cm.
The Museum of Modern Art, New
York. Gift of Walter P. Chrysler, Jr.

p 60
Sleeping Peasants. Paris, 1919.
Tempera, watercolor, and pencil,
31.1 × 48.9 cm.
The Museum of Modern Art, New
York. Abby Aldrich Rockefeller Fund.

p 61
**Woman in Spanish Costume
(La Salchichona).** Barcelona, 1917.
Oil on canvas, 116 × 89 cm.
Museo Picasso, Barcelona.

p 62
Three Women at the Spring.
Fontainebleau, Summer 1921.
Oil on canvas, 203.9 × 174 cm.
The Museum of Modern Art,
New York. Gift of Mr. and Mrs. Allan
D. Emil.

p 63
**Harlequin (Portrait of the Painter
Jacint Salvadó).** Paris, 1923.
Oil on canvas, 130 × 97 cm.
Musée National d'Art Moderne,
Centre Georges Pompidou, Paris.

p 64
Paulo as Harlequin. Paris, 1924.
Oil on canvas, 130 × 97 cm.
Musée Picasso, Paris.

p 65
Bather with Beach Ball. Boisgeloup,
August 30, 1932.
Oil on canvas, 146.2 × 114.6 cm.
The Museum of Modern Art, New
York. Mr. and Mrs. Joseph H. Lauder
Collection.

pp 66-67
Guernica. May 1–June 4, 1937.
Oil on canvas, 349.3 × 776.6 cm.
Museo Nacional Centro de Arte
Reina Sofía, Madrid.

p 68
Weeping Woman. Paris, October 26,
1937.
Oil on canvas, 60 × 49 cm.
The Tate Gallery, London.

p 69
Woman Dressing Her Hair. Royan,
June 1940.
Oil on canvas, 130 × 97 cm.
Private Collection, New York.

p 70
The Studio of La Californie. Cannes,
March 30, 1956.
Oil on canvas, 114 × 146 cm.
Musée Picasso, Paris.

p 71
**The Maids of Honor (Las Meninas),
after Velázquez.** Cannes,
September 4, 1957.
Oil on canvas, 46 × 37.5 cm.
Museu Picasso, Barcelona.

p 71
Las Meninas (The Doves, 1).
Cannes, September 7, 1957.
Oil on canvas, 100 × 80 cm.
Museu Picasso, Barcelona.

p 72
The Maids of Honor (Las Meninas).
Cannes, November 17, 1957.
Oil on canvas, 35 × 27 cm.
Museu Picasso Barcelona.

p 73
Las Meninas (Isabel de Velasco).
Cannes, December 30, 1957.
Oil on canvas, 33 × 24 cm.
Museu Picasso, Barcelona.

p 74
Luncheon on the Grass, after Manet.
Vauvenargues, March 3–August 20,
1960.
Oil on canvas, 130 × 195 cm.
Musée Picasso, Paris.

p 75
Woman with Hat. 1962.
Linoleum cut, 63.5 × 52.5 cm.
Museu Picasso, Barcelona.

p 76
Character. Mougins, January 19,
1972.
Oil on canvas, 100 × 81 cm.
Private Collection.

p 77
Head of a Man. Mougins, April 30,
1972.
Oil on canvas, 81 × 65 cm.
Private Collection.

SELECTED BIBLIOGRAPHY

JOSEP PALAU I FABRE. *The Early
Years. 1881 - 1907.* Barcelona:
Ediciones Polígrafa, 1980.

KLAUS GELLWITZ. *Picasso 1945-
1973.* Paris: Denoël, 1986.

PICASSO. *Écrits.* Paris: Gallimard,
1989.

JOSEP PALAU I FABRE. *Picasso
cubism. 1907-1917.* Barcelona:
Ediciones Polígrafa, 1990.

PIERRE CABANNE. *Le Siècle de
Picasso.* Paris: Gallimard-Folio, 1992.

JOSEP PALAU I FABRE. *From the
Ballets to Drama. 1917-1926.*
Barcelona: Ediciones Polígrafa, 1999.

JOSEP PALAU I FABRE. *Ultimate
Picasso.* Barcelona: Ediciones
Polígrafa, 2000.